D1715123

HELLO FRIENDS! I'M COACH NINA. WELCOME TO THE TENNIS LESSONS FOR BEGINNERS. OVER THE NEXT FEW MONTHS I WILL BE YOUR TENNIS COACH. WORDS CANNOT DESCRIBE HOW THRILLED I AM ABOUT IT. BUT BEFORE WE START, I WOULD LIKE FOR YOU TO LEARN A LITTLE BIT ABOUT ME.

GROWING UP, MY PARENTS KEPT ME BUSY WITH SPORTS. I TRIED EVERYTHING FROM GYMNASTICS TO TAEKWONDO TO SWIMMING. THEN, ONE SUMMER DAY I DISCOVERED TENNIS. IT WAS LOVE AT FIRST SIGHT.

I WAS BORN AND RAISED IN A SMALL TOWN IN SIBERIA. TENNIS COACHES WEREN'T PLENTIFUL AROUND THERE AT THE TIME. SO MY DAD JUST SAID: "GO PLAY AGAINST THE WALL." AND I DID. WHEN HE HAD TIME, HE WOULD TEACH ME THINGS THAT HE OBSERVED OTHERS DO. HE DIDN'T KNOW THE FIRST THING ABOUT TENNIS BUT HE DID HIS BEST TO LEARN AND TEACH ME.

FINALLY, MY DAD FOUND A GOOD COACH WHO, ALTHOUGH RELUCTANTLY, BUT SIGNED ME UP FOR CLASSES. TENNIS TURNED OUT TO BE A GREAT SPORT FOR ME. I LEARNED THE TECHNIQUE PRETTY FAST AND BY NEXT YEAR I STARTED TO PARTICIPATE IN THE TOURNAMENTS. I WOULD SPEND COUNTLESS HOURS ON THE COURT, PRACTICING MY STROKES AND PLAYING WITH ANYONE WILLING TO PLAY. ANOTHER YEAR LATER I WAS WINNING MATCHES AGAINST SOME OF THE BEST PLAYERS IN MY STATE FOR MY AGE LEVEL. EVERY WEEKEND, RAIN OR SHINE, MY DAD WOULD COME OUT TO PLAY WITH ME. HE ALWAYS HAD SOME VALUABLE INSIGHTS.

TENNIS WAS A MAJOR PART OF MY LIFE THROUGHOUT MY SCHOOL YEARS. HOWEVER, DUE TO SOME DIFFICULTIES I COULD NOT PURSUE A PROFESSIONAL CAREER IN TENNIS AFTER GRADUATING HIGH SCHOOL.

WHEN I BECAME A MOM FOR THE FIRST TIME, I WANTED TO BUILD A STRONGER BOND WITH MY SON AND FIND ACTIVITIES THAT WE WOULD BOTH ENJOY. NATURALLY, I INTRODUCED HIM TO TENNIS. AS I TAUGHT MY SON DIFFERENT STROKES, QUITE OFTEN, OTHER FAMILIES WOULD COME UP AND ASK ME TO COACH THEIR KIDS. I REALIZED THAT I LIKE TO SHARE MY KNOWLEDGE AND EXPERIENCE WITH CHILDREN AND THEIR PARENTS. ALTHOUGH I HAVEN'T CONSIDERED IT BEFORE, IT INSPIRED ME TO BECOME A USPTA CERTIFIED TENNIS COACH.

TENNIS HAS BEEN MY PASSION FOR OVER 25 YEARS. I FELL IN LOVE WITH THE SPORT AND HAVE BEEN PLAYING IT SINCE I WAS A KID. I HAVE GAINED A LOT OF EXPERIENCE FROM TRAINING PEOPLE AND NOW I WOULD LIKE TO SHARE IT WITH YOU. THAT'S WHY I CREATED THIS WORKBOOK WITH A STEP-BY-STEP LESSONS THAT PARENTS CAN USE TO TEACH THEIR KIDS TO PLAY THIS WONDERFUL GAME.

HOW TO USE THIS WORKBOOK

I AM SO HAPPY THAT YOU TOOK INTEREST IN LEARNING THE GAME OF TENNIS. I AM HONORED THAT YOU CHOSE THIS WORKBOOK TO BE YOUR GUIDE IN THE WORLD OF TENNIS.

THIS EXERCISE BOOK IS INTENDED FOR PARENTS AND THEIR CHILDREN, SIBLINGS, FRIENDS, AND SPOUSES. IT WAS WRITTEN TO TEACH YOU HOW TO RALLY AND AS A SOURCE TO ENRICH YOUR WEEKENDS WITH ENJOYABLE FAMILY ACTIVITIES. MOREOVER, EVEN NOVICE COACHES WILL BENEFIT FROM THIS BOOK BY FINDING FUN GAME IDEAS AND EXERCISES TO INCORPORATE INTO THEIR CLASSES. BEFORE YOU START WITH THE LESSONS, THOUGH, I WOULD LIKE TO PROVIDE AN OVERVIEW AND MY RECOMMENDATIONS FOR CERTAIN PARTS OF THE BOOK.

FIRST THINGS FIRST, PLEASE WRITE A LETTER TO YOUR FUTURE SELF AND ASSESS YOUR CURRENT FORM.

TO HELP YOU DEVELOP AND STICK WITH GOOD HABITS, I'VE INCLUDED SEVERAL TRACKERS. THESE WILL HELP YOU STAY GROUNDED TOWARD YOUR GOALS. IF YOU EVER FEEL LIKE GIVING UP, THERE'S A MOTIVATIONAL LETTER. PERHAPS IT WILL INSPIRE YOU TO KEEP GOING.

TENNIS HAS A UNIQUE SCORING SYSTEM, TRADITIONS, AND VOCABULARY. IT'S NOT SURPRISING SINCE THE SPORT HAS SUCH A RICH HISTORY. A PRIMITIVE VARIANT OF TENNIS WAS PLAYED BY THE ANCIENT GREEKS AND ROMANS OVER TWO THOUSAND YEARS AGO. LATER, DURING THE MIDDLE AGES, ROYAL FAMILIES IN FRANCE AND ENGLAND ENJOYED A MORE DEVELOPED FORM OF THIS SPORT. FINALLY, MODERN TENNIS AS WE KNOW IT TODAY EVOLVED FROM "THE GAME OF PALM" THAT WAS INVENTED IN ENGLAND IN 1873. THUS, BEFORE YOU DIVE INTO THE LESSONS, FAMILIARIZE YOURSELF WITH RULES, TERMINOLOGY AND COURT ETIQUETTE. THIS WILL HELP YOU TO FEEL EVEN MORE CONFIDENT ON THE COURT.

DEVELOPED TO PROVIDE HANDS-ON SUPPORT FOR THE BEGINNING PLAYER, THIS WORKBOOK IS CHOCK FULL OF HELPFUL INFORMATION AND EXERCISES. EVERYTHING FROM REACTION TIME AND BALL CONTROL TO HAND-EYE COORDINATION AND FOOTWORK WILL BE COVERED IN DETAIL FOR A LEARNING EXPERIENCE YOU'LL LOVE. PLAYERS OF ALL LEVELS WORK ON THOSE SKILLS TO STAY SHARP AND READY TO TAKE ON ANY OPPONENT. THE LESSONS ARE STRUCTURED SO THAT YOU CAN LEARN THEM ALL AND HONE YOUR TECHNIQUE THROUGH PRACTICE.

AND THE MOST IMPORTANT PART - THE FIFTEEN LESSONS THAT YOU WILL FIND ON THE PAGES INSIDE, ARE INTENDED TO BE REPEATED AS MANY TIMES AS NEEDED UNTIL THE SKILLS IN THAT LESSON ARE MASTERED.

MOST OF THE LESSONS AND DRILLS IN THIS WORKBOOK CAN BE ADAPTED FOR EITHER INDIVIDUAL CLASSES OR SMALL GROUP (UP TO FOUR PLAYERS) LESSONS. YOU CAN ALSO TAILOR THE LENGTH OF THE LESSONS FROM 30 MINUTES TO AN HOUR LONG BY ADJUSTING THE AMOUNT OF DRILLS AND REPETITIONS.

VISUALIZE YOUR SUCCESS AS A PLAYER. IT WON'T BE LONG BEFORE YOU START COLLECTING YOUR FIRST VICTORIES.

BEST OF LUCK,
XOXO, COACH NINA.

QUESTIONS TO CONSIDER BEFORE STARTING TO PRACTICE

PREVIOUS TENNIS TEACHERS. WHAT DID I / MY CHILD LEARNED FROM HIM?
....
....

HOW DID I / MY CHILD LIKED HIS TEACHING STYLE? ....
....
....

THINGS I / MY CHILD ENJOYED THE MOST ABOUT HIS CLASSES? ....
....
....

HOW DO YOU / YOUR CHILD RATE YOURSELF AS A PLAYER?

1	2	3	4	5	6	7	8	9	10

WHAT OTHER SPORTS DID (DO) YOU / YOUR CHILD PLAY (ED)? ....
....
....

HOW OFTEN WOULD YOU LIKE TO PLAY WITH OTHER PEOPLE? HOW MANY TIMES A WEEK?

S	M	T	W	TH	F	S

HOW OFTEN DO YOU PLAN TO PRACTICE? HOW MANY TIMES A WEEK?

S	M	T	W	TH	F	S

MY GOALS AND OBJECTIVES? ....
....
....
....
....
....
....
....
....

ASSESSMENT OF A PLAYER'S SKILLS AND ABILITIES

WHEN STUDENTS FIRST COME TO MY CLASSES, WE DO AN INITIAL ASSESSMENT OF THEIR SKILLS AND ABILITIES. THIS IS DONE NOT TO COMPARE A BEGINNER PLAYER AGAINST THE STANDARD NORMS BUT TO RECORD AND KEEP THE INITIAL RESULTS. HOW MUCH HE/SHE CAN IMPROVE IN A CERTAIN TIME FRAME. THIS IS DONE MORE SO TO TEACH KIDS TO SET UP MINI GOALS AND REACH IT.

NOW, I'D LIKE FOR YOU TO DO THE SAME. BELOW IS A LIST OF EXERCISES THAT I WOULD LIKE FOR YOU (YOUR CHILD) TO DO (AND KEEP THE RECORD OF) BEFORE STARTING THIS PROGRAM.

1. RUN ONE LAP AROUND THE COURT AS FAST AS POSSIBLE ON TIME. COACH STARTS THE TIMER.

BEFORE   AFTER

2. HOW MANY TIMES CAN A PLAYER SKIP ON A JUMP ROPE UNINTERRUPTED IN ONE MINUTE?

BEFORE   AFTER

3. SHUFFLE NON-STOP FOR 30 SECONDS FROM THE CENTER OF THE SERVICE LINE TO THE SINGLES LINE. COUNT EVERY TIME YOU STEP ON THE LINE.

BEFORE   AFTER

4. HOW MANY PUSH UPS CAN A PLAYER DO IN ONE MINUTE?

BEFORE   AFTER

5. STANDING LONG JUMP.
FROM A STANDING POSITION, FEET SLIGHTLY APART AND PARALLEL TO EACH OTHER. JUMP AS FAR FORWARD AS POSSIBLE. THE RESULT IS MEASURED FROM THE TOES TO THE HEELS AFTER LANDING.

BEFORE   AFTER

6. HIGH KNEES FOR 30 SECONDS NON-STOP.

BEFORE   AFTER

THESE AND MANY OTHER EXERCISES AND DRILLS WE WILL BE ADDING TO OUR CLASSES.

FIRST ASSIGNMENT FOR THE PLAYER

I KNOW THAT YOU CANNOT WAIT TO GET OUT TO THE TENNIS COURT AND START YOUR FIRST PRACTICE. BUT BEFORE YOU DO THAT, PLEASE DO ONE WRITTEN ASSIGNMENT.

I WOULD LIKE FOR YOU TO TRAVEL IN TIME AND PRETEND THAT YOU ALREADY KNOW HOW TO PLAY TENNIS, SERVE AN ACE, AND HIT A BACKHAND DOWN THE LINE. THE JOURNEY HAS BEEN LONG AND FILLED WITH SACRIFICE, BUT YOU'VE MADE IT. HOW DOES IT MAKE YOU FEEL? WHAT THOUGHTS RUN THROUGH YOUR MIND? ARE YOU HAPPY THAT YOU EMBARKED ON THIS JOURNEY?

NOW GET A PEN AND WRITE A LETTER TO YOURSELF. WRITE DOWN ALL THE HARD WORK THAT YOU THINK THAT YOU ARE GOING TO HAVE TO DO, EMOTIONS AND FEELINGS THAT YOU MIGHT EXPERIENCE WHILE REACHING YOUR GOALS, AS WELL AS ALL THE FUN YOU'LL HAVE ALONG THE WAY. BE KIND BUT FIRM AND ENCOURAGE YOURSELF TO STAY STRONG, DISCIPLINED, AND TO NOT GIVE UP.
IN THE FUTURE, WHEN THINGS GET OVERWHELMING, SOME EXERCISES BECOME DIFFICULT, AND YOU FEEL LIKE GIVING UP, YOU CAN READ THIS LETTER AND REMIND YOURSELF WHY YOU STARTED THIS JOURNEY.

....
....
....
....
....
....
....
....
....
....
....
....
....
....
....
....
....
....
....
....
....
....
....
....
....
....
....
....

HABITS TRACKERS

OVER THE NEXT FEW MONTHS, YOU ARE GOING TO LEARN NEW THINGS AND ADOPT NEW HABITS.

SLEEP

PEOPLE SPEND A THIRD OF THEIR LIVES IN BED. SLEEP IS VITAL FOR OUR WELLBEING, ESPECIALLY FOR CHILDREN. DURING SLEEPING HOURS A GROWTH HORMONE IS RELEASED, BODIES RESTORE ENERGY AND BRAIN SORTS THROUGH A LOT OF INFORMATION.

WATER

OUR BODIES ARE MADE UP OF 70% WATER. THAT'S WHY IT'S IMPORTANT TO DRINK FRESH, CLEAN WATER, NOT SODAS OR COFFEE. PROPER WATER INTAKE IS IMPORTANT FOR EVERYONE, AND NOT JUST ATHLETES.

FOOD

IN THIS WORKBOOK I WOULD LIKE FOR YOU TO TRACK THE FOODS THAT YOU EAT. WE ARE NOT GOING TO GET INTO THE DETAILS OF AN ATHLETE'S NUTRITION. HOWEVER, I WOULD STILL RECOMMEND TO CUT BACK ON JUNK FOOD, SODAS AND SWEETS.

RUN OR WALK

IT IS RECOMMENDED THAT KIDS RUN OR WALK AT LEAST A MILE EVERY DAY. THEREFORE, BESIDES TENNIS TRAINING, IT'S IMPORTANT TO GET IN AT LEAST 5000 STEPS A DAY. KEEP TRACK OF IT HERE.

EXERCISE

HERE YOU CAN KEEP YOUR EXERCISE CALENDAR. YOU CAN KEEP TRACK OF NOT ONLY TENNIS PRACTICES BUT ALSO OTHER FITNESS ACTIVITIES THAT YOU ENJOY (RIDING A BIKE, SWIMMING, PLAYING SOCCER, ETC.)

EACH OF THESE ASPECTS ARE IMPORTANT AND WILL HELP TO ESTABLISH A NEW SCHEDULE AND TRACK YOUR ACCOMPLISHMENTS IN TENNIS AND IN LIFE.

STAY CONSISTENT AND TRACK PROGRESS EVERY DAY. IN A MONTH YOU WILL SEE WHAT A DIFFERENCE SMALL STEPS CAN MAKE.

NOTES: . . . .
. . . .
. . . .
. . . .
. . . .
. . . .
. . . .
. . . .
. . . .
. . . .

BEDTIME TRACKER

MORE INFORMATION ABOUT THE BENEFITS OF SLEEP YOU CAN FIND HERE

DATE: ..|..|..   ..|..|..   ..|..|..   ..|..|..   ..|..|..   ..|..|..   ..|..|..

_____   _____   _____   _____   _____   _____   _____
_____   _____   _____   _____   _____   _____   _____

DATE: ..|..|..   ..|..|..   ..|..|..   ..|..|..   ..|..|..   ..|..|..   ..|..|..

_____   _____   _____   _____   _____   _____   _____
_____   _____   _____   _____   _____   _____   _____

DATE: ..|..|..   ..|..|..   ..|..|..   ..|..|..   ..|..|..   ..|..|..   ..|..|..

_____   _____   _____   _____   _____   _____   _____
_____   _____   _____   _____   _____   _____   _____

DATE: ..|..|..   ..|..|..   ..|..|..   ..|..|..   ..|..|..   ..|..|..   ..|..|..

_____   _____   _____   _____   _____   _____   _____
_____   _____   _____   _____   _____   _____   _____

DATE: ..|..|..   ..|..|..   ..|..|..   ..|..|..   ..|..|..   ..|..|..   ..|..|..

_____   _____   _____   _____   _____   _____   _____
_____   _____   _____   _____   _____   _____   _____

NOTES:...
....
....
....
....
....
....

WATER TRACKER
FOR 21 DAYS

1/2 OZ   X   1 LB   =   "N" OZ

WATER INTAKE CALCULATOR

1
2
3
4
5
6
7
8
9
10
11
12
13
14
15
16
17
18
19
20
21

JUNK FOOD TRACKER

YOU CAN ALWAYS FIND MORE
INFORMATION ABOUT PROTEIN, HEALTHY
FATS AND CARBOHYDRATES HERE.

DATE: ..|..|.. ..|..|.. ..|..|.. ..|..|.. ..|..|.. ..|..|.. ..|..|..

DATE: ..|..|.. ..|..|.. ..|..|.. ..|..|.. ..|..|.. ..|..|.. ..|..|..

DATE: ..|..|.. ..|..|.. ..|..|.. ..|..|.. ..|..|.. ..|..|.. ..|..|..

DATE: ..|..|.. ..|..|.. ..|..|.. ..|..|.. ..|..|.. ..|..|.. ..|..|..

DATE: ..|..|.. ..|..|.. ..|..|.. ..|..|.. ..|..|.. ..|..|.. ..|..|..

NOTES: ....
....
....
....
....
....
....
....
....
....
....
....
....
....

STEPS TRACKER

COLOR IN AND RECORD THE STEPS

ONE WAY

- 5 000   - 10 000

DATE: ..|..|..   ..|..|..   ..|..|..   ..|..|..   ..|..|..   ..|..|..   ..|..|..

DATE: ..|..|..   ..|..|..   ..|..|..   ..|..|..   ..|..|..   ..|..|..   ..|..|..

DATE: ..|..|..   ..|..|..   ..|..|..   ..|..|..   ..|..|..   ..|..|..   ..|..|..

DATE: ..|..|..   ..|..|..   ..|..|..   ..|..|..   ..|..|..   ..|..|..   ..|..|..

DATE: ..|..|..   ..|..|..   ..|..|..   ..|..|..   ..|..|..   ..|..|..   ..|..|..

DATE: ..|..|..   ..|..|..   ..|..|..   ..|..|..   ..|..|..   ..|..|..   ..|..|..

NOTES: ....
....
....
....
....
....
....
....
....
....
....
....
....

APPS

OLDER KIDS AND PARENTS CAN ALSO TRACK PROGRESS AND NEW HABITS ONLINE. THERE ARE A LOT OF APPLICATIONS THAT CAN HELP YOU TRACK, CONTROL AND REMIND TO KEEP UP WITH THE NEW HABITS AND ROUTINES.

 APPLE WATCH - TRACKS YOUR ACTIVITY THROUGHOUT THE DAY. KEEPS TRACK OF YOUR SLEEP, STEPS, FITNESS LEVEL AND CAN BE PAIRED WITH OTHER APPS TO MONITOR YOUR HEART RATE.

 HYDRO COACH - AN APPLICATION THAT HELPS TO SET UP A DAILY WATER INTAKE GOAL AND WILL REMIND YOU DURING THE DAY TO HYDRATE.

 HEADSPACE - AN APPLICATION WITH OVER 500 MEDITATIONS THAT WILL HELP YOU UNWIND AT THE END OF THE DAY AND CALM YOUR MIND BEFORE GOING TO BED. IT CAN ALSO HELP KIDS TO DEAL WITH ANXIETY AND OVERSTIMULATION BEFORE BEDTIME.

 HABITICA - IS A VIDEO GAME INSPIRED APPLICATION THAT HELPS PEOPLE TO STICK WITH NEW HABITS. EVERY TIME YOU ACHIEVE A NEW GOAL, IT PROMOTES YOU TO THE NEXT LEVEL AND AWARDS A NEW AVATAR. OLDER KIDS MAY FIND IT ENGAGING.

 MYFITNESSPAL - THIS IS PROBABLY THE BEST CALORIE COUNTING APPLICATION ON THE MARKET. IT HAS A BIG DATABASE OF FOODS INCLUDING FROM DIFFERENT RESTAURANTS. YOU CAN ALSO ADD YOUR OWN RECIPES AND IT WILL CALCULATE CARBS, FATS AND PROTEIN ALONE WITH CALORIES.

 RUNKEEPER - AN APP THAT TRACKS DISTANCE, TIME AND CALORIES BURNED DURING A RUN. IT ALSO OFFERS A VARIETY OF RUNNING ROUTES IN YOUR AREA AS WELL AS WORKS WITH OTHER APPS.

 DON'T FORGET TO UTILIZE ALL THE BUILT-IN OPTIONS ON YOUR PHONE. SET UP A
- **SLEEP MODE TO GET AN UNINTERRUPTED GOOD NIGHT'S SLEEP.**
- **CALENDAR TO KEEP UP WITH THE PRACTICES, EVENTS AND GOALS.**
- **TIMER-USE IT DURING THE PRACTICE TO TRACK YOUR SPEED AND TIME.**

NOTES: . . . .
. . . .
. . . .
. . . .
. . . .
. . . .
. . . .

PRACTICE TRACKER

WRITE DOWN AND TRACK YOUR PRACTICE SCHEDULE ....
....
....
....

PRACTICE:	S	M	T	W	TH	F	S
	○	○	○	○	○	○	○
	○	○	○	○	○	○	○
	○	○	○	○	○	○	○
	○	○	○	○	○	○	○
	○	○	○	○	○	○	○
	○	○	○	○	○	○	○

■ ● ▲ MONDAY
....
....
....
....
....
....
....
....

■ ● ▲ TUESDAY
....
....
....
....
....
....
....
....

■ ● ▲ WEDNESDAY
....
....
....
....
....
....
....
....

■ ● ▲ THURSDAY
....
....
....
....
....
....
....
....

■ ● ▲ FRIDAY
....
....
....
....
....
....
....
....

■ ● ▲ SATURDAY
....
....
....
....
....
....
....
....

MOTIVATION

THERE IS NO GREAT ACHIEVEMENT THAT DOES NOT INVOLVE GREAT EFFORT. IN LIFE, AS IN TENNIS, THE SAME RULE HOLDS TRUE. COUNTLESS HOURS ON THE COURT, BREAKING SWEAT EVERY DAY, TRIAL AND ERROR SUMS UP THE CHALLENGES OF EVERYDAY LIFE: A PERSON HAS TO LOVE WHAT S(HE) DOES. THERE SHOULD BE A BURNING INNER DESIRE TO COME OUT ON THE COURT AND ENJOY EVERY SUCCESS AND EVERY FAILURE.

BUT TRUTH BE KNOWN, NOT ALL PEOPLE, ESPECIALLY KIDS, CAN BE SO SELF-MOTIVATED. WHEN PEOPLE TRY NEW THINGS, LIKE A NEW SPORT, MAJORITY DOESN'T SUCCEED IMMEDIATELY. IT TAKES TIME TO LEARN AND FULLY UNDERSTAND WHETHER IT IS SOMETHING THAT YOU OR YOUR CHILD CAN STICK WITH. WHEN STROKES AREN'T PERFECT, AND A PERSON HAVE TAKEN FIVE CLASSES ALREADY, S(HE) MAY START TO LOSE INTEREST AND GIVE UP. WHEN IT COMES TO KIDS, THE MOST IMPORTANT THING TO REMEMBER IS THAT THE ACTIVITIES SHOULD BE FUN.

SO, NEXT TIME YOUR KIDS (ADULTS TOO) HESITATE TO GO TO PLAY TENNIS, CONSIDER THIS:

1. KIDS LEARN BY WATCHING PARENTS AND OLDER SIBLINGS. COME OUT AND PLAY WITH YOUR KIDS. THAT'S WHY I CAME UP WITH THIS WORKBOOK IN THE FIRST PLACE - YOU CAN BOTH LEARN THE GAME AND HAVE FUN DOING IT. WHEN KIDS SENSE THEIR PARENTS' ENTHUSIASM, ALL THEY WOULD WANT TO DO IS KEEP PLAYING IT AGAIN AND AGAIN.

2. INVITE FRIENDS AND SIBLINGS TO JOIN THE GAME. AT THIS AGE, DOING ACTIVITIES WITH OTHER KIDS ADDS JOY AND DRIVE TO THE SPORT.

3. IF YOUR CHILD LIKES TO COMPETE, CREATE CHALLENGING GAMES, RELAY RALLIES, AND FRIENDLY MATCHES AMONGST FAMILY AND FRIENDS.

4. SET GOALS. YOU CAN EVEN SIGN A COMMITMENT CONTRACT WITH YOUR CHILD. BEYOND TENNIS, THIS WILL TEACH THEM RESPONSIBILITY AND RELIABILITY.

NOTES: ....
....
....
....
....
....
....
....
....
....
....
....
....
....
....

IT'S TOUGH TO MAKE SOMEBODY DO THINGS THAT THEY DON'T LIKE. ESPECIALLY KIDS. MAKE SPORTS EXCITING FOR YOU AND YOUR KIDS, AND BEFORE LONG, THEY WILL BE THRILLED TO GO TO THE TENNIS COURT.

EQUIPMENT THAT YOU ARE GOING TO NEED

PLAYERS OF DIFFERENT AGES ARE GOING TO NEED EQUIPMENT OF DIFFERENT SIZES. FOR REFERENCE, PLEASE SEE THE TABLE BELOW.

AGE:		HEIGHT:	RACKET SIZE:	TENNIS BALLS:
4 - 5 YEARS		3'6"	19"	LARGE FOAM
6 - 7 YEARS		4'0"	21"	RED BALL
7 - 8 YEARS		4'3"	23"	ORANGE BALL
9 - 10 YEARS		4'5"	25"	GREEN DOT
10 - 12 YEARS		4'6"+	26"	YELLOW BALL
13+ YEARS		4'6"+	27"	YELLOW BALL

CHECK LIST:

- [ ] TENNIS BALLS - 100 MIN
- [ ] TENNIS RACKET
- [ ] TENNIS SHOES
- [ ] JUMP ROPE
- [ ] VISOR
- [ ] SUNSCREEN
- [ ] TOWEL
- [ ] WATER
- [ ] HAIR TIE
- [ ] SPOT MARKERS
- [ ] CONES
- [ ] BEAN BAG
- [ ] REACTION BALL
- [ ] LADDER

NOTES: . . . .
. . . .
. . . .
. . . .
. . . .

TENNIS COURT

COURT LENGTH: 78 FT.

NET

DOUBLES ALLEY			39 FT. X 4.5 FT. (175.5 SQ. FT)	
BASELINE / CENTRE MARK	NO MAN'S LAND	SERVICE LINE	AD COURT LEFT SERVICE BOX — 21 FT. X 13.5 FT. (283.5 SQ. FT)	18 FT. X 27 FT. (486 SQ. FT.)
			CENTRE SERVICE LINE	
			DEUCE COURT RIGHT SERVICE BOX — 21 FT. X 13.5 FT. (283.5 SQ. FT)	
SINGLES SIDELINE				
DOUBLES SIDELINE			39 FT. X 4.5 FT. (175.5 SQ. FT.)	

COURT WIDTH: 36 FT.

NET POST

TYPE OF SURFACE

THERE ARE THREE MAIN TYPES OF TENNIS COURT SURFACE. EACH ONE IS UNIQUE AND OFFERS DIFFERENT ADVANTAGES AND CHALLENGES.

GRASS IS THE FASTEST SURFACE AVAILABLE. THE BALL BOUNCES LOW AND FAST. GRASS IS VERY DEPENDENT ON THE WEATHER. EVEN IN A SLIGHT DRIZZLE THE SURFACE BECOMES SLIPPERY WHICH RAISES A RISK OF GETTING INJURED.

CLAY IS MY FAVORITE. THE BALLS BOUNCE HIGH AND SLOW. THE SURFACE IS GENTLE ON THE JOINTS. PERFECT FOR PLAYERS WHO LIKE TO STAY AT THE BASELINE. BESIDES, IT'S MORE ECOLOGICAL AND NON-TOXIC.

HARD COURT OFFERS THE MIDDLE GROUND BETWEEN CLAY AND GRASS. IT'S NEITHER FAST NOR SLOW. PRETTY EASY AND INEXPENSIVE TO MAINTAIN AND LONG LASTING.

NOTES: . . . .
. . . .
. . . .
. . . .
. . . .
. . . .

TENNIS RULES
SCORING 101 CHEAT SHEET

MATCH:
COMPOSED OF SETS
MUST WIN 2 OUT OF 3 OR 3 OUT OF 5 SETS

NOTES:

SETS:
COMPOSED OF GAMES
PLAYERS ALTERNATE THE SERVICE EVERY GAME
MUST WIN 6 GAMES AND LEAD BY 2
A TIEBREAK IS PLAYED AT 6 GAMES ALL
PRO SET IS PLAYED TO 8 GAMES, WIN BY 2

TIEBREAK:
FIRST PLAYER TO 7 POINTS AHEAD BY 2, WINS
A PLAYER WHO RETURNED THE PREVIOUS GAME, SERVES FIRST
SERVING STARTS TO THE AD-COURT
SWITCH ENDS EVERY 6 POINTS

GAMES:
CONSIST OF POINTS
ONE PLAYER SERVES THE ENTIRE GAME
MUST WIN 4 POINTS, AHEAD BY 2

POINTS:
1 - 15, 2 - 30, 3 - 40, 0 - LOVE
IF THE SAME NUMBER OF POINTS, SAY ALL
(FOR EXAMPLE, 15 - ALL)

DEUCE:
40 - 40 OR 40 ALL
SERVER'S ADVANTAGE "AD IN"
RETURNER'S ADVANTAGE "AD OUT"
MUST WIN BY 2

COMPETITION FORMATS FOR BEGINNER PLAYERS

BEGINNER PLAYERS NEED A LOT OF PRACTICE COMPETITION TO OVERCOME FEAR, NERVOUSNESS AND OTHER EMOTIONS. THE BEST WAY TO LEARN TO PLAY AGAINST A VARIETY OF DIFFERENT PEOPLE WITH DIFFERENT PLAYING STYLES, IS IN A FRIENDLY AND FUN ATMOSPHERE. TOURNAMENT ORGANIZERS LIKE TO MAKE COMPETITION AN ENJOYABLE EXPERIENCE FOR ALL PLAYERS, HENCE A VARIETY OF COMPETITION FORMATS HAVE BEEN ADDED. HERE IT IS:

1. ONE SHORT SET - THE FIRST PLAYER TO WIN FOUR GAMES, WINS.

2. ROUND ROBIN - EACH PLAYER GETS TO PLAY AGAINST EVERYONE IN THEIR GROUP.

3. TIEBREAK INSTEAD OF A THIRD SET.

4. BEST OF THREE SHORT SETS - THE FIRST PLAYER TO WIN TWO SHORT SETS (4 GAMES), WINS A MATCH.

5. NO AD - SCORING - INSTEAD OF PLAYING AD IN/AD OUT, A DECISIVE POINT IS PLAYED AT 40-40 (DEUCE).

6. BEST OF THREE MATCH TIEBREAK - INSTEAD OF PLAYING SHORT GAMES, TIEBREAKS ARE PLAYED. THE FIRST ONE TO WIN TWO TIEBREAKS WINS A MATCH.

ALSO, A COMBINATION OF THESE FORMATS CAN BE PLAYED.

NOTES: . . . .
. . . .
. . . .
. . . .
. . . .
. . . .
. . . .
. . . .
. . . .
. . . .
. . . .
. . . .
. . . .
. . . .
. . . .
. . . .
. . . .
. . . .
. . . .
. . . .
. . . .
. . . .
. . . .
. . . .
. . . .

TENNIS COURT ETIQUETTE

THE FIRST RULE OF TENNIS STATES: TREAT YOUR OPPONENT WITH COURTESY AND RESPECT. GOOD MANNERS AND COMMON SENSE ARE THE BASIS FOR TENNIS ETIQUETTE.

PLAYERS

1. FIRST THINGS FIRST, WHEN YOU COME TO THE TENNIS COURT, WHETHER TO PRACTICE OR PLAY A MATCH, TURN YOUR CELL PHONE OFF. IF YOUR PHONE RINGS DURING THE PRACTICE, IT'S DISRESPECTFUL TO THE COACH OR YOUR PARTNER. IF IT RINGS DURING A MATCH, AN OPPONENT CAN CLAIM THE POINT AS AN INTENTIONAL DETERRENT. BESIDES, IT CAN DISTRACT YOU FROM FOCUSING ON THE GAME.

PLAYERS

2. BEFORE EVERY MATCH, PLAYERS HAVE FIVE (5) MINUTES TO WARM UP. USE THIS TIME TO RALLY WITH YOUR OPPONENT, HIT DIFFERENT TYPES OF STROKES AS WELL AS HELP YOUR OPPONENT TO WARM UP. THERE'S NO NEED TO HIT WINNERS OR IMPRESS YOUR OPPONENT WITH YOUR SKILLS. YOU WILL HAVE PLENTY OF OPPORTUNITIES TO DO SO DURING THE MATCH.

PLAYERS

3. WHEN WARMING UP THE SERVICE, CATCH THE BALLS INSTEAD OF RETURNING IT.

PLAYERS

4. WHEN PLAYING A MATCH WITHOUT OFFICIALS:

NOTES:.............................
....
....
....
....
....
....
....
....
....
....
....

PLAYERS

A) EACH PLAYER SHOULD ANNOUNCE THE SCORE BEFORE THEY SERVE. THE SCORE OF THE SET SHOULD BE CALLED OUT BEFORE EVERY GAME. THE SCORE OF THE GAME SHOULD BE CALLED OUT BEFORE EVERY POINT.

PLAYERS

B) TRY NOT TO QUESTION LINE CALLS. IT IS A GOOD IDEA TO GIVE CREDIT TO THE OPPONENT IF YOU ARE UNSURE IF THE BALL WENT IN OR OUT. ALWAYS BE HONEST AND FAIR WHEN YOU HAVE TO MAKE A LINE CALL.

PLAYERS

5. REFRAIN FROM TALKING, SCREAMING OR INTENTIONAL VISUAL DISTRACTION DURING A POINT. THIS DISTRACTS YOU AND YOUR OPPONENT. BESIDES, YOU CAN LOSE A POINT BECAUSE OF IT.

PLAYERS

6. IF YOUR OPPONENT HIT A SERVICE OUT, TRY NOT TO RETURN IT. AS TEMPTED YOU MAY BE BY THROWING THEIR RHYTHM OFF, DON'T DO IT. INSTEAD, EITHER PUT THAT BALL IN YOUR POCKET OR TOSS IT TO THE CORNER.

PLAYERS

7. CLEAR OUT ALL THE BALLS BEFORE EVERY POINT. BOTH PLAYERS SHOULD MAKE SURE THAT THERE ARE NO BALLS TO DISTRACT THEM FROM PLAYING. THE ONLY EXCEPTION IS IF A BALL IS STUCK AT THE BOTTOM OF THE NET.

PLAYERS

8. IF YOUR BALLS ROLLED OVER TO THE NEIGHBORING COURT, STAY AND WAIT ON YOUR COURT UNTIL THOSE PLAYERS FINISH THE POINT AND THEN YOU CAN GO GET IT BACK. OTHERWISE, YOU MAY DISTRACT THEM, GET HIT WITH A BALL OR A RACKET AND LEARN A LOT OF NEW THINGS ABOUT YOURSELF.

PLAYERS

9. IF YOU HIT A BALL AND IT HITS THE NET AND LANDS ON YOUR OPPONENT SIDE OF THE COURT, IT'S PURE LUCK. TENNIS PLAYERS HAVE A TRADITION TO WAVE BACK AT THE OPPONENT AS A SIGN OF RECOGNITION. THOSE MOMENTS ARE FRUSTRATING AND THE LEAST YOU CAN DO IS TO APOLOGIZE AND RECOGNIZE THAT YOU GOT LUCKY.

PLAYERS

10. AFTER THE MATCH, IT IS CUSTOMARY FOR TENNIS PLAYERS TO SHAKE HANDS AND LOOK EACH OTHER IN THE EYES. IT'S A GOOD IDEA TO EITHER CONGRATULATE THEM ON A WIN OR OFFER ENCOURAGEMENT IF THEY LOST.

PLAYERS

11. MAKE SURE THAT YOU WEAR AN APPROPRIATE ATTIRE FOR THE TENNIS COURT. AN IMPORTANT THING TO REMEMBER IS TO WEAR TENNIS SHOES WITH NON-MARKING SOLES. SOME CLUBS HAVE IT AS A REQUIREMENT.

SPECTATORS.

1. DURING A MATCH, SPECTATORS SHOULD BE QUIET.

2. CHEERING AND CLAPPING IS ENCOURAGED AFTER THE POINT IS FINISHED BUT NOT WHILE THEY PLAY.

PARENTS.

1. DURING A MATCH, AVOID SHOWING YOUR EMOTIONS. THIS MAY DISTRACT BOTH PLAYERS AND YOU MAY BE ASKED TO LEAVE THE BLEACHERS.

2. DON'T GET INVOLVED IN THE MATCH. TEACH YOUR CHILD TO KEEP SCORE AND ASK OFFICIALS FOR HELP IF THERE'S A DISAGREEMENT ABOUT A LINE CALL.

THERE YOU HAVE IT. NEXT TIME YOU ARE ON THE COURT, REMEMBER TO ENCOURAGE YOUR OPPONENT AND DO NOT SHOW SIGNS OF FRUSTRATION. ALTHOUGH, THERE ARE A LOT MORE ETIQUETTE RULES, THESE ARE A GOOD START.

3. DURING THE PRACTICE, DON'T ROLL OR HIT THE BALLS TO THE COACH. HE OR SHE IS FOCUSED ON YOUR CHILD, AND MAY NOT NOTICE AND STEP ON THE BALL OR EVEN WORSE, YOU MAY HIT A COACH WITH A BALL.

VOCABULARY

IF YOU EVER WATCHED A TENNIS MATCH, YOU MAY HAVE NOTICED THAT TENNIS LINGO CAN BE CONFUSING. TO HEP YOU BETTER NAVIGATE AROUND A TENNIS COURT, I PUT TOGETHER A SHORT LIST OF WORDS THAT ARE COMMONLY USED BY TENNIS PLAYERS. IT WILL ALSO HELP YOU TO UNDERSTAND THE LANGUAGE IN THIS WORKBOOK BETTER.

ACE – A BALL THAT IS SERVED SO WELL THE OPPONENT CANNOT TOUCH IT WITH THEIR RACQUET.

AD – SHORT FOR ADVANTAGE. IT IS THE POINT SCORED AFTER DEUCE. IF THE SERVING SIDE SCORES, IT IS AD-IN. IF THE RECEIVING SIDE SCORES, IT IS AD-OUT.

ALL – AN EVEN SCORE. 30-30 IS, FOR EXAMPLE, 30-ALL.

BACKHAND – THE STROKE USED TO RETURN BALLS HIT TO THE LEFT SIDE OF A RIGHT-HANDED PLAYER (OR TO THE RIGHT SIDE OF A LEFT-HANDED PLAYER). BACKHANDS ARE HIT EITHER ONE-HANDED OR TWO-HANDED.

DEUCE – A SCORE OF 40-ALL, OR 40-40. THIS MEANS THAT THE SCORE IS TIED AND EACH SIDE HAS WON AT LEAST THREE POINTS.

DEUCE COURT – THE RIGHT SIDE OF THE COURT, SO CALLED BECAUSE ON A DEUCE SCORE, THE BALL IS SERVED THERE.

DOUBLE FAULT – FAILURE OF BOTH SERVICE ATTEMPTS. ON A DOUBLE FAULT, THE SERVER LOSES THE POINT.

DOUBLES – A MATCH WITH FOUR PLAYERS, TWO ON EACH TEAM.

FAULT – A SERVED BALL THAT DOES NOT LAND IN THE PROPER SERVICE BOX.

FOOT FAULT – A FAULT CALLED AGAINST THE SERVER FOR STEPPING ON OR OVER THE BASELINE WITH EITHER FOOT DURING DELIVERY OF THE SERVE.

FOREHAND – A STROKE HIT WITH A DOMINANT HAND. IF A PLAYER IS RIGHT HAND DOMINANT, THEN FOREHAND IS PLAYED ON THE RIGHT HAND SIDE (OR TO THE LEFT SIDE IF A PLAYER IS LEFT-HANDED). FOREHANDS ARE COMMONLY HIT ONE-HANDED.

GAME – THE PART OF A SET THAT IS COMPLETED WHEN ONE PLAYER OR SIDE EITHER WINS FOUR POINTS AND IS AT LEAST TWO POINTS AHEAD OF HIS OR HER OPPONENT, OR WHO WINS TWO POINTS IN A ROW AFTER DEUCE.

GROUND STROKE – A STROKE MADE AFTER THE BALL HAS BOUNCED; EITHER A FOREHAND OR BACKHAND.

LET – A POINT PLAYED OVER BECAUSE OF INTERFERENCE. ALSO, A SERVE THAT HITS THE TOP OF THE NET BUT IS OTHERWISE GOOD, IN WHICH CASE THE SERVE IS TAKEN AGAIN.

NO-AD – A SYSTEM OF SCORING A GAME IN WHICH THE FIRST PLAYER TO WIN FOUR POINTS WINS THE GAME. IF THE SCORE REACHES 3-ALL, THE NEXT POINT DECIDES THE GAME.

NO MAN'S LAND – A SLANG TERM FOR THE AREA BETWEEN THE SERVICE LINE AND THE BASELINE.

OUT – A BALL LANDING OUTSIDE THE BOUNDARY LINES OF THE COURT.

POINT – THE SMALLEST UNIT OF SCORING.

RALLY – A SERIES OF GOOD HITS MADE SUCCESSFULLY BY PLAYERS. ALSO, THE PRACTICE PROCEDURE IN WHICH PLAYERS HIT THE BALL BACK AND FORTH TO EACH OTHER.

RECEIVER – THE PLAYER WHO RECEIVES THE SERVE. ALSO KNOWN AS THE RETURNER.

SERVE – SHORT FOR SERVICE. IT IS THE ACT OF PUTTING THE BALL INTO PLAY FOR EACH POINT.

SERVER – THE PLAYER WHO SERVES.

SET – A SCORING UNIT AWARDED TO A PLAYER WHO OR TEAM THAT HAS WON: (A) 6 OR MORE GAMES AND HAS A TWO-GAME LEAD; OR (B) 6 GAMES AND THE TIEBREAK GAME WHEN PLAYED AT 6-ALL.

STROKE – AN ACT OF STRIKING THE BALL WITH THE RACQUET.

TIEBREAK – A SYSTEM IN TRADITIONAL TENNIS USED TO DECIDE A SET WHEN THE SCORE IS TIED, 6-ALL.

VOLLEY – DURING PLAY, A STROKE MADE BY HITTING THE BALL BEFORE IT HAS TOUCHED THE GROUND.

NOTES: . . . .
. . . .
. . . .
. . . .
. . . .
. . . .
. . . .

REACTION BALL

REACTION BALLS ARE USED IN A NUMBER OF SPORTS, SUCH AS TENNIS, BASKETBALL AND BASEBALL. IT IS USED TO TRAIN HAND-EYE COORDINATION, AGILITY, FAST THINKING AND IMPROVE REACTION TIME.

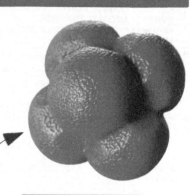

REACTION BALL IS MADE OF RUBBER, BRIGHTLY COLORED AND LOOKS LIKE A BUNCH OF BALLS MELTED TOGETHER. IT IS DONE THIS WAY SO THAT WHEN IT BOUNCES, A PLAYER CANNOT PREDICT WHICH WAY IT WILL GO.

YOU CAN USE IT ON YOUR OWN TO BOUNCE OFF THE WALL OR MAKE IT MORE FUN AND PLAY WITH FAMILY AND FRIENDS. JUST TAKE TURNS BOUNCING IT OFF THE FLOOR AND WATCH EACH OTHER RUN IN DIFFERENT DIRECTIONS. THIS MAKES FOR A GREAT WORKOUT.

NOTES: ....
....
....
....
....
....
....
....
....
....
....
....
....

REACTION TIME

MODERN TENNIS HAS BECOME VERY FAST. TECHNOLOGY THAT IS USED IN RACKETS, STRINGS, BALLS AND COURT SURFACES CONTRIBUTE HIGHLY TO THE SPEED OF THE GAME. EVEN AMATEUR PLAYERS HIT FASTER SERVES AND GROUND STROKES.

AN UNPREPARED PLAYER WITH SLOW REACTION CAN GET FRUSTRATED QUICKLY. LUCKILY, REACTION TIME CAN BE TRAINED AND IMPROVED. IT REQUIRES WORK AND DEDICATION BUT THE BENEFITS EXTEND FAR BEYOND THE TENNIS COURT.

BELOW IS A LIST OF EXERCISES THAT WILL HELP YOU TO DEVELOP A FASTER REACTION TIME.
I RECOMMEND TO DO EACH EXERCISE FOR 30 SECONDS AT A TIME, 2-3 SETS EACH.

1. UTILIZE A REACTION BALL. HAVE A COACH DROP A BALL IN FRONT OF A PLAYER AT RANDOM. A PLAYER HAS TO CATCH IT AFTER ONE BOUNCE. THIS IS A DIFFICULT EXERCISE AND IT CAN GET FRUSTRATING, BUT KEEP DOING IT, YOU WILL GET IT.

2. HAVE A PLAYER STAND IN FRONT OF A COACH FACING BACKWARDS. A COACH THROWS OR ROLLS BALLS FROM BEHIND A PLAYER TO THE FRONT OF A PLAYER IN DIFFERENT DIRECTIONS AT DIFFERENT SPEEDS. A PLAYER HAS TO CATCH IT AS FAST AS POSSIBLE, ONCE HE SEES IT.

3. A PLAYER AND A COACH STAND IN FRONT OF EACH OTHER, SEVERAL FEET APART. A COACH HOLDS TWO BALLS AND DROPS IT IN FRONT OF HIM AT RANDOM. A PLAYER HAS TO CATCH IT AFTER ONE BOUNCE.

4. AGAIN, A PLAYER AND A COACH STAND IN FRONT OF EACH OTHER, ARM'S LENGTH AWAY. A COACH HOLDS TWO BALLS, ONE IN EACH HAND. ARMS ARE IN FRONT OF HIM. A PLAYER KEEPS HIS/HER HANDS NEAR COACH'S HANDS. A COACH DROPS BALLS AT RANDOM ONE AT TIME OR BOTH AT THE SAME TIME AND A PLAYER HAS TO CATCH IT BEFORE IT BOUNCES OFF THE COURT.

5. A COACH AND A PLAYER STAND IN FRONT OF A WALL, A PLAYER CLOSER IS TO THE WALL, A COACH IS A FEW FEET BEHIND A PLAYER. A COACH THROWS A BALL AT THE WALL. A PLAYER HAS TO CATCH IT AFTER IT BOUNCES OFF THE WALL AND OFF THE COURT ONCE. YOU CAN CHALLENGE YOURSELF AND CATCH A BALL BEFORE IT BOUNCES OFF THE COURT.

NOTES: . . . .
. . . .
. . . .
. . . .
. . . .
. . . .
. . . .
. . . .
. . . .
. . . .
. . . .

TO SEE THE DEMONSTRATION OF EXERCISES AND DRILLS, PLEASE SCAN THE QR CODE.

6. DODGEBALL. A PLAYER STANDS CLOSE TO THE WALL FACING A COACH. A COACH THROWS BALLS AT THE WALL WHILE TRYING TO HIT A PLAYER. A PLAYER HAS TO MOVE FAST FROM SIDE TO SIDE TO AVOID GETTING HIT.

7. A PLAYER STANDS CLOSE TO THE WALL FACING A COACH. A COACH STANDS IN FRONT OF A PLAYER. A COACH TOSSES BALLS AT A PLAYER, ONE AT A TIME. A PLAYER HAS TO CATCH THE BALLS AND TOSS IT BACK TO THE COACH.

8. A PLAYER STANDS AT THE BASELINE WITH HIS BACK FACING A COACH. A COACH IS AT THE SERVICE LINE TOSSES ONE BALL AT A TIME UP IN THE AIR AND SAYS "GO". A PLAYER HAS TO TURN AROUND AND RUN AND CATCH A BALL AFTER THE FIRST BOUNCE.

9. A COACH AND A PLAYER EACH HOLD A BALL. BOTH ARE TOSSING BALLS AT THE SAME TIME IN DIFFERENT DIRECTIONS, BUT SO, THAT IT STAYS WITHIN THE BOUNDARIES OF A SERVICE BOX. BOTH A PLAYER AND A COACH RUN AND CATCH EACH OTHER'S BALLS BEFORE IT BOUNCES TWICE. THIS IS A FUN GAME TO PLAY WITH YOUR CHILD.

10. SET UP FOUR CONES A FEW FEET AWAY FROM EACH OTHER IN A SQUARE. A PLAYER STANDS IN THE MIDDLE OF THE SQUARE. A COACH POINTS AT THE CONE AND A PLAYER HAS TO RUN FAST AND TAP IT WITH HIS/HER HAND.

BALL CONTROL

THERE ARE A FEW DIFFERENT BALL CONTROLS IN TENNIS. AS A BEGINNER, A BALL PLACEMENT IS THE ONE THAT WE ARE GOING TO FOCUS ON. ONCE YOU ARE ABLE TO RALLY, THE NEXT STEP IS TO LEARN TO HIT A BALL IN A WAY THAT IS DIFFICULT FOR YOUR OPPONENT TO RETURN.

I INCLUDED BALL CONTROL EXERCISES STARTING WITH LESSON 10. AS WITH EVERYTHING, WE ARE GOING TO START EASY AND WORK OUR WAY UP. IF SOME EXERCISES ARE TOO DIFFICULT, KNOW THAT IT'S TEMPORARY. THE MORE YOU WORK ON IT THE FASTER YOU WILL MASTER IT.
GOOD LUCK!

NOTES: . . . .
. . . .
. . . .
. . . .
. . . .
. . . .
. . . .
. . . .
. . . .
. . . .
. . . .
. . . .
. . . .
. . . .

HAND-EYE COORDINATION

DRILLS WITH A RACKET AND A BALL.

1. SET UP SIX (6) CONES (OR BALL CANS) ABOUT TWO-THREE FEET APART ALONG A SIDE LINE. USING ONE BALL AND A RACKET LEAD THE BALL IN A SNAKE PATTERN AROUND THE CONES ONE WAY AND THEN BACK.

2. PUT A BALL ON THE RACKET AND HAVE A PLAYER WALK IN A SNAKE PATTERN AROUND THE CONES. THE GOAL HERE IS TO KEEP THE BALL ON THE RACKET AND NOT LET IT ROLL OFF OF IT.

3. DRIBBLE THE BALL OFF THE COURT WITH A RACKET FOR ONE (1) MINUTE.

4. BOUNCE THE BALL OFF THE RACKET FOR ONE (1) MINUTE.

5. FRYING PAN WITH A BEAN BAG (BEGINNER) OR A TENNIS BALL (MORE ADVANCED). IT CAN BE PLAYED IN A GROUP OR BETWEEN TWO PEOPLE (PLAYER AND A COACH). IT CAN BE PLAYED IN A CIRCLE OR OVER THE NET.

DRILLS WITH A BALL.

1. RUN AROUND THE COURT AND DRIBBLE THE BALL WITH A HAND.

2. HOLD TWO BALLS, ONE IN EACH HAND. DRIBBLE ONE BALL WITH A DOMINANT HAND FIVE TIMES AND THEN DROP AND CATCH A BALL WITH A NON-DOMINANT HAND. REPEAT 5 TIMES.

3. A PLAYER STARTS IN THE MIDDLE OF THE BASELINE. A COACH/PARTNER TOSSES A BALL GENTLY TO FOREHAND AND BACKHAND SIDES. A PLAYER SHUFFLES FROM SIDE TO SIDE TO CATCH A BALL AFTER IT BOUNCES ONCE. TOSSES IT BACK TO THE COACH.

4. THE SAME SET UP AS IN THE PREVIOUS DRILL, EXCEPT THIS TIME, A PLAYER CATCHES A BALL BEFORE IT BOUNCES OFF THE COURT. TOSSES IT BACK TO THE COACH.

5. JUGGLING. START WITH TWO BALLS. ONCE YOU MASTER THAT, ADD A THIRD BALL.

NOTES: . . . .
. . . .
. . . .
. . . .
. . . .
. . . .
. . . .
. . . .
. . . .
. . . .

DRILLS USING A TENNIS WALL.

1. THE SIMPLEST ONE IS TO TOSS A BALL AGAINST THE WALL AND CATCHING IT WITH BOTH HANDS.

2. MAKE IT A LITTLE HARDER AND CATCH IT WITH ONE HAND AT A TIME.

3. TOSS A BALL AGAINST A WALL WITH YOUR RIGHT HAND AND CATCH IT WITH LEFT ONE. REPEAT FOR 30 SECONDS.

4. SET UP TARGETS (SPOT MARKERS OR BALLOONS, OR A COUPLE OF PIECES OF PAPER) ON A WALL. ALTERNATE TOSSING BALLS AT THE TARGET BETWEEN RIGHT AND LEFT HANDS.

5. USING A RACKET, HIT BALLS AGAINST THE WALL WITH DIFFERENT STRENGTH. START CLOSE TO THE WALL AND HIT EASY BALLS. THEN MOVE BACK A COUPLE OF STEPS. CONTINUE TO MOVE BACK A FEW TIMES. THEN START TO MOVE FORWARD A COUPLE OF STEPS AT A TIME UNTIL YOU GET TO THE INITIAL SPOT.

NOTES:. . . . .

TO SEE THE DEMONSTRATION OF EXERCISES AND DRILLS, PLEASE SCAN THE QR CODE.

ANALYSIS OF GRIPS

ONE OF THE FIRST THINGS THAT PEOPLE LEARN WHEN THEY COME TO THE TENNIS COURT IS HOW TO HOLD A RACKET. THERE ARE 6 MAIN GRIPS FOR RIGHT-HANDED AND LEFT HAND DOMINANT PEOPLE. BELOW WE ARE GOING TO ANALYZE HOW TO HOLD EACH GRIP, THEIR PROS AND CONS . . . .
. . . .
. . . .
. . . .

MAIN POINTS ON THE HAND

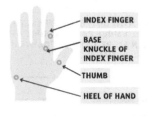

- INDEX FINGER
- BASE KNUCKLE OF INDEX FINGER
- THUMB
- HEEL OF HAND

BUTT

1 - TOP
2 - RIGHT BEVEL
3 - RIGHT VERTICAL PANEL
4 - RIGHT UNDER BEVEL
5 - BOTTOM
6 - LEFT UNDER BEVEL
7 - LEFT VERTICAL PANEL
8 - LEFT BEVEL

WHEN WE HOLD A RACKET, THERE ARE TWO MAIN POINTS ON THE HAND TO KEEP IN MIND. IT IS UNDERSIDE OF A BASE KNUCKLE ON THE INDEX FINGER AND A HEEL OF THE HAND. WHEN WE PLAY, WE NEED THESE POINTS TO ALIGN A CERTAIN WAY WITH THE BEVELS ON THE RACKET. THE REASON FOR THAT IS IT ALLOWS US TO CHANGE THE GRIPS BY MOVING HANDS SLIGHTLY.

DURING THE FIRST FEW CLASSES, I ENCOURAGE YOU TO REFER TO THIS PART TO MEMORIZE HOW TO HOLD A RACKET FOR DIFFERENT SHOTS.

HOW DO YOU DECIDE WHICH GRIP IS RIGHT FOR YOU? EVERY PLAYER IS BUILT SLIGHTLY DIFFERENT, EVERYONE IS UNIQUE WITH THEIR STRONG AND WEAK SIDES. THE ONLY WAY TO FIGURE OUT WHAT IS RIGHT FOR YOU IS TO TRY ALL THE GRIPS AND DECIDE WHICH ONE FEELS RIGHT.

FOR THE BEGINNER PLAYERS I WOULD RECOMMEND TO START WITH THE FOLLOWING GRIPS:

- FOREHAND - SEMI-WESTERN.
- BACKHAND - TWO HANDED BACKHAND.
- SERVICE, VOLLEY AND SLICE - CONTINENTAL GRIP.

NOTES: . . . .
. . . .
. . . .
. . . .
. . . .
. . . .
. . . .

1. EASTERN FOREHAND GRIP

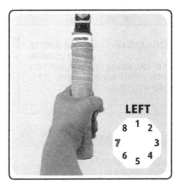

LEFT

8 1 2
7 ⬡ 3
6 5 4

RIGHT

8 1 2
7 ⬡ 3
6 5 4

■ ● ▲

EASTERN GRIP IS ALSO CALLED A "SHAKE HANDS" GRIP. FOR RIGHT HAND DOMINANT PLAYERS THE BASE KNUCKLE OF THE INDEX FINGER AND A HEEL OF THE HAND ARE PLACED ON BEVEL 3. FOR LEFTIES, PLACE IT ON BEVEL 7.

■ ● ▲ ADVANTAGES

- EASY TO GENERATE TOPSPIN
- WAIST-HIGH BALLS
- ADAPTABLE TO DIFFERENT SURFACES
- MORE SUPPORT
- TOPSPIN
- GOOD FOR BEGINNERS SINCE IT PROMOTES GOOD CONTACT

■ ● ▲ DISADVANTAGES

- REQUIRES A GRIP CHANGE
- WEAK ON SLICE
- LOW VOLLEY
- FINESSE AND TOUCH SHOTS
- DIFFICULT TO HIT HIGH BALLS

NOTES: ....
....
....
....
....
....
....
....
....
....
....
....
....
....
....
....
....
....

2. EASTERN BACKHAND GRIP

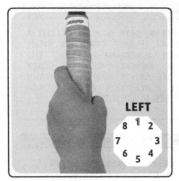

LEFT

```
  8  1  2
 7        3
  6  5  4
```

RIGHT

```
  8  1  2
 7        3
  6  5  4
```

■ ● ▲

THE KNUCKLE OF THE INDEX FINGER AND A HEEL OF THE HAND ARE BOTH PLACED ON BEVEL 1. THIS APPLIES TO BOTH RIGHT-HANDED AND LEFT-HANDED PLAYERS.

■ ● ▲   **ADVANTAGES**

- EASY TO GENERATE POWER
- WAIST-HIGH BALLS
- ADAPTABLE TO DIFFERENT SURFACES
- MORE SUPPORT
- TOPSPIN
- GOOD FOR BEGINNERS SINCE IT PROMOTES GOOD CONTACT

■ ● ▲   **DISADVANTAGES**

- REQUIRES A GRIP CHANGE
- WEAK ON SLICE
- LOW VOLLEY
- FINESSE AND TOUCH SHOTS
- DIFFICULT TO HIT HIGH BALLS

NOTES: ....
....
....
....
....
....
....
....
....
....
....
....
....
....
....
....
....

3. CONTINENTAL GRIP

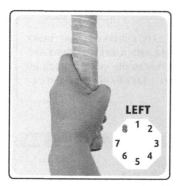

LEFT

8 1 2
7 · 3
6 5 4

■ ● ▲

THE BASE KNUCKLE OF THE INDEX FINGER AND A HEEL OF THE HAND ARE PLACED ON RIGHT-HANDED - BEVEL 2, LEFT-HANDED - BEVEL 8.

■ ● ▲ **ADVANTAGES**

- LOW BALLS
- SLICE
- NO GRIP CHANGE
- ADAPTABLE TO DIFFERENT STROKES
- DEGREE OF VERSATILITY
- TOPSPIN ON SERVE
- LATE HIT ON FOREHAND SIDE
- GOOD SERVE AND VOLLEY
- GOOD FOR HIT TOUCH SHOTS

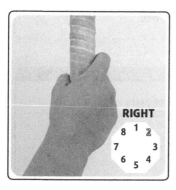

RIGHT

8 1 2
7 · 3
6 5 4

■ ● ▲ **DISADVANTAGES**

- HIGH BALLS
- MORE DIFFICULT TO GENERATE TOPSPIN THAN EASTERN GRIP
- REQUIRES GOOD TIMING

NOTES: ....
....
....
....
....
....
....
....
....
....
....
....
....
....
....
....
....

4. SEMIWESTERN FOREHAND

LEFT

```
   1
 8   2
7     3
 6   4
   5
```

■ ● ▲

THE BASE KNUCKLE OF THE INDEX FINGER AND A HEEL OF THE HAND ARE PLACED ON: RIGHT-HANDED ON BEVEL 4, LEFT-HANDED ON BEVEL 6.

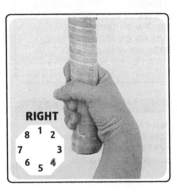

RIGHT

```
   1
 8   2
7     3
 6   4
   5
```

■ ● ▲   **ADVANTAGES**

- TOPSPIN
- HIGH BALLS
- DISGUISE
- PASSING SHOTS
- POWER

■ ● ▲   **DISADVANTAGES**

- LOW BALLS
- UNDERSPIN
- MAJOR GRIP CHANGE TO BACKHAND
- SERVE
- LOW VOLLEY

NOTES: ....
....
....
....
....
....
....
....
....
....
....
....
....
....
....
....

5. FULL WESTERN FOREHAND

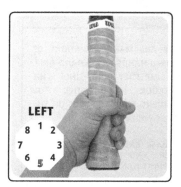

LEFT

■ ● ▲

THE BASE KNUCKLE OF THE INDEX FINGER AND A HEEL OF THE HAND ARE PLACED ON BEVEL 5. IT IS THE SAME FOR RIGHTIES AND LEFTIES.

■ ● ▲ ADVANTAGES

- TOPSPIN
- HIGH BALLS
- DISGUISE
- PASSING SHOTS
- POWER

RIGHT

■ ● ▲ DISADVANTAGES

- LOW BALLS
- UNDERSPIN
- MAJOR GRIP CHANGE TO BACKHAND
- SERVE
- LOW VOLLEY

NOTES: ....
....
....
....
....
....
....
....
....
....
....
....
....
....
....
....
....
....

6. TWO-HANDED BACKHAND

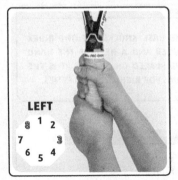

LEFT

RIGHT

■ ● ▲

THERE ARE MANY VARIATIONS OF THE TWO-HANDED BACKHAND GRIP. FOR SIMPLICITY AND SINCE THIS WORKBOOK IS INTENDED FOR BEGINNERS, WE WILL FOCUS ON THE EASIEST VARIATION.

THE BASE KNUCKLE OF THE INDEX FINGER AND A HEEL OF THE DOMINANT HAND ARE PLACED ON:

RIGHTIES - BEVEL 2. LEFT HAND IS ON BEVEL 7. RIGHT HAND IS ON THE BOTTOM OF THE HANDLE. LEFT HAND IS AT THE TOP OF THE HANDLE, CLOSER TO THE THROAT OF THE RACKET.

LEFTIES - BEVEL 8. LEFT HAND IS ON BEVEL 3. LEFT HAND IS ON THE BOTTOM OF THE HANDLE. RIGHT HAND IS AT THE TOP OF THE HANDLE, CLOSER TO THE THROAT OF THE RACKET.

■ ● ▲   **ADVANTAGES**

- TOPSPIN
- HIGH BALLS
- DISGUISE
- PASSING SHOTS
- POWER

■ ● ▲   **DISADVANTAGES**

- LOW BALLS
- UNDERSPIN
- MAJOR GRIP CHANGE TO BACKHAND
- SERVE
- LOW VOLLEY

NOTES: . . . .
. . . .
. . . .
. . . .
. . . .
. . . .
. . . .
. . . .
. . . .
. . . .
. . . .
. . . .
. . . .
. . . .
. . . .
. . . .
. . . .
. . . .

WARM UP

TENNIS IS ONE OF THOSE SPORTS WHERE GETTING INJURED IS RELATIVELY EASY. THE MOST COMMON INJURIES AMONGST AMATEUR PLAYERS ARE TENNIS ELBOW, SPRAINED ANKLES AND MUSCLE STRAINS. TO MINIMIZE THE RISK OF THESE INJURIES, IT IS RECOMMENDED TO DO A GOOD WARM UP AND STRETCHING BEFORE AND AFTER EVERY PRACTICE OR A MATCH. LISTED BELOW ARE SOME OF THE EXERCISES THAT PLAYERS SHOULD INCLUDE IN THEIR WARM UP ROUTINES.

TO SEE THE DEMONSTRATION OF EXERCISES AND DRILLS, PLEASE SCAN THE QR CODE.

....
....
....
....

1) LIGHT JOGGING AROUND THE TENNIS COURT 3-5 LAPS

2) JUMP OVER A LINE FEET MOVING LIKE SCISSORS - 40 SECS

3) SHUFFLING - 30 SECS

4) JUMP ON RIGHT FOOT - 30 SECS

5) JUMPING JACKS - 30 SECS - 1 MIN

6) JUMP ON LEFT FOOT - 30 SECS

7) BACKPEDALING - 30 SECS

8) BUTT KICKS - 30 SECS

9) HIGH KNEES - 30 SECS

**10) DUCK WALK
- ALONG THE SIDELINE**

**11) CRAB WALK
- ALONG THE SIDELINE**

**12) ARM ROTATION
FORWARD - 10 TIMES**

**13) ARM ROTATION
BACKWARD - 10 TIMES**

**14) ELBOW ROTATION
INWARD - 10 TIMES**

**15) WRIST ROTATIONS
- 10 TIMES**

**16) ELBOW ROTATION
OUTWARD - 10 TIMES**

**17) JUMP ROPE -
1 - 2,5 MINS**

**18) CARIOCA -
ALONG A SIDELINE**

**19) JUMP OVER A LINE
WITH BOTH FEET**

20) SKIPS - 10 TIMES

21) LUNGES SIDEWAYS - 10 TIMES

22) BEAR CRAWL - ALONG A SIDELINE

....
....
....
....
....
....
....
....

STRETCHING AND COOL DOWN

TENNIS IS A FUN SPORT. PEOPLE OF ALL AGES ENJOY THIS GAME. HOWEVER, IT CAN BE VERY DEMANDING. ALONE WITH MAJOR MUSCLES A LOT OF SMALLER MUSCLES ARE USED TO HIT VOLLEYS, FOREHANDS AND SERVES. IF NOT PROPERLY TAKEN CARE OF, IT'S VERY EASY TO GET INJURED. THAT'S WHY, TENNIS PLAYERS SHOULD MAKE IT A HABIT TO STRETCH BEFORE AND AFTER EACH PRACTICE OR A MATCH.

HERE I WOULD LIKE TO OFFER YOU A FEW STRETCHING EXERCISES THAT ARE PARTICULARLY GOOD FOR TENNIS PLAYERS.

BEFORE

AFTER A WARM UP AND BEFORE YOU START TO PLAY, SPEND A FEW MINUTES TO STRETCH YOUR:

- WRISTS BY HOLDING YOUR ARM STRAIGHT IN FRONT OF YOU AND USING THE OTHER HAND TO HELP GENTLY PUSH IT DOWN. HOLD FOR A FEW SECONDS.
- BRING YOUR ARMS AND HANDS BEHIND YOUR BACK IN A LOCK. HOLD FOR 5-10 SECONDS. SWITCH ARMS.
- HIPS. PUT YOUR FEET AS FAR APART AS POSSIBLE (LATERAL LUNGE), BEND YOUR KNEES AND MOVE SIDE TO SIDE GIVING THE MUSCLES A GOOD STRETCH.
- FEET. DON'T FORGET ABOUT ANKLES AND ACHILLES' TENDON. PUT ONE FOOT AT A TIME AGAINST THE FENCE OR A BENCH AND PUT SOME WEIGHT FORWARD.
- FOR THIS STRETCH EXERCISE YOU CAN USE A RACKET OR A JUMP ROPE FOLDED IN HALF TWICE. KEEP ELBOWS STRAIGHT, TAKE THE RACKET BEHIND YOUR BACK AND BRING IT FORWARD. REPEAT 5 TIMES.

AFTER

AFTER THE MATCH OR A PRACTICE STRETCH YOUR:

- QUADRICEPS - BRING YOUR FOOT TO YOUR BOTTOM AND GIVE IT A GOOD STRETCH.
- TRUNK AND BACK - LAY DOWN ON THE GROUND ON YOUR BACK. ARMS TO THE SIDES. BEND YOUR KNEES AND TURN IT TO ONE SIDE. TURN YOUR HEAD TO THE OTHER SIDE. HOLD FOR A FEW SECONDS. CHANGE SIDES.
- HAMSTRINGS - WHILE LAYING ON THE GROUND, PICK THE RIGHT LEG UP AND EXTEND IT. LEFT LEG IS BENT. HOLD FOR 10-15 SECONDS. SWITCH LEGS.
- HAMSTRINGS - STAND UP STRAIGHT, FEET TOGETHER. BEND OVER AND REACH FOR YOUR KNEES WITH YOUR FOREHEAD. HOLD ON THIS POSITION FOR A FEW SECONDS.

EVERY TIME AFTER YOU FINISH YOUR PRACTICE, DON'T FORGET TO JOG AROUND THE COURT SLOWLY TO COOL DOWN AND STRETCH YOUR BODY TO AVOID TIGHTNESS AND UNPLEASANT SENSATIONS IN YOUR MUSCLES. TRY NOT TO SKIP THESE STEPS AS IT WILL HELP YOU RECOVER FASTER AND PREVENT INJURIES. ....
....
....
....

TO SEE THE DEMONSTRATION OF EXERCISES AND DRILLS, PLEASE SCAN THE QR CODE.

FOREHAND

THE FIRST STROKE I WOULD LIKE FOR YOU TO LEARN IS A FOREHAND. IT IS PROBABLY THE EASIEST STROKE IN TENNIS. IT CAN ALSO BECOME ONE OF YOUR STRONGEST WEAPONS ON THE COURT.

A COUPLE OF DISCLAIMERS.

- THIS TECHNIQUE IS FOR BEGINNERS.
- THE MOVEMENTS DESCRIBED ARE FOR RIGHT-HAND DOMINANT PLAYERS. LEFTIES SHOULD USE THE OPPOSITE ARMS AND FEET.
- AS BEGINNERS WE ARE LEARNING A CLOSED STANCE.

GRIP. MY FAVORITE GRIP FOR A FOREHAND STROKE IS SEMI-WESTERN. HOWEVER, IT MAY BE A LITTLE DIFFICULT AT FIRST. IF THAT'S THE CASE, I RECOMMEND TO USE AN EASTERN GRIP. SEE PAGE 23 FOR INFORMATION ABOUT GRIPS.

SWING. ROTATE YOUR UPPER AND LOWER BODY PARTS TO THE RIGHT (LEFT FOR LEFTIES).

FIRST TIME

IF IT'S YOUR FIRST TIME PLAYING TENNIS - JUST EXTEND YOUR ELBOW TO THE SIDE AND DROP THE RACKET HEAD DOWN. CHECK AND MAKE SURE THAT THE RACKET IS NOT BEHIND YOUR BACK, BUT RATHER TO YOUR SIDE.

IF YOU PLAYED A LITTLE BIT BEFORE

AS YOU ROTATE YOUR SHOULDERS TO THE SIDE, MAKE A LOOP WITH YOUR RACKET AS IF YOU DRAW A RAINBOW. KEEP ELBOWS AWAY FROM YOUR BODY. NOW EXTEND YOUR ARM AND DROP THE RACKET HEAD DOWN.
QUICK TIP. WHEN HITTING A BALL, THE RACKET HEAD SHOULD TRAVEL FROM BOTTOM (BELOW THE BALL) TO THE TOP.

FEET. KEEP YOUR KNEES BENT. HEELS OFF THE COURT , ALL THE BODY WEIGHT SHOULD BE ON THE BALLS OF THE FEET. MAKE SMALL STEPS AS YOU GET READY TO HIT THE BALL.

WEIGHT TRANSFER.

IN ORDER TO HIT A STRONG SHOT, A PLAYER NEEDS TO ADD A BODY WEIGHT TO THE STROKE. FOR THAT, POINT TO THE BALL WITH YOUR LEFT HAND, BRING YOUR LEFT FOOT FORWARD TOWARDS THE BALL AND SET IT ON YOUR HEEL FIRST AND THEN ROLL THE REST OF THE FOOT. NOW YOU ARE READY TO HIT THE BALL. EXTEND YOUR KNEES, TRANSFER THE WEIGHT TO THE LEFT LEG AND HIT THE BALL WITH AN EXTENDED ELBOW IN FRONT OF YOU.

POINT OF CONTACT.

ONCE THE BALL BOUNCES OFF THE COURT, YOU SHOULD HIT IT ON THE SIDE AND IN FRONT OF YOU. TRY TO EXTEND YOUR ELBOW AS MUCH AS POSSIBLE, TO THE POINT WHERE IT'S ALMOST STRAIGHT. THE HEAD OF THE RACKET SHOULD BE PARALLEL OR SLIGHTLY OPEN AND LOOK UP WHEN HITTING A BALL. IF IT LOOKS DOWN, ALL THE BALLS ARE GOING TO END UP AT THE NET.

FOLLOW THROUGH.

AS YOU FINISH UP THE STROKE, YOUR RIGHT HAND SHOULD MOVE IN THE SAME WAY AS IF YOU TURN A DOOR KNOB TO THE LEFT. DON'T STOP THE RACKET AFTER YOU HIT THE BALL, INSTEAD KEEP THE MOMENTUM GOING AND MOVE IT TO THE LEFT SHOULDER. CATCH THE RACKET WITH THE LEFT HAND FOR SUPPORT. THIS MOVEMENT IS CALLED A FOLLOW THROUGH.

SO HERE YOU GO. A STEP BY STEP EXPLANATION OF THE FOREHAND STROKE FOR A BEGINNER PLAYER. NOW YOU SHOULD HIT 1000 SHOTS TO MEMORIZE THIS MOVEMENT.

TWO-HANDED BACKHAND

TWO-HANDED BACKHAND IS A GROUND STROKE THAT IS HIT BY THE NON-DOMINANT HAND WITH THE SUPPORT OF THE DOMINANT ARM. TECHNIQUE DESCRIBED BELOW IS INTENDED FOR A BEGINNER PLAYER.

GRIP. I SUGGEST YOU USE EASTERN GRIP FOR YOUR LEFT HAND (KNUCKLE OF THE INDEX FINGER AND A HEEL OF THE HAND ARE PLACED ON BEVEL 7), AND CONTINENTAL GRIP FOR YOUR DOMINANT HAND. MORE INFORMATION ABOUT THE GRIPS YOU CAN FIND ON PAGE 31.

SWING.

WITH THE BACKHAND, WE NEED TO TAKE THE NON-DOMINANT ARM BACK AS FAR AS POSSIBLE IN ORDER TO ACCELERATE IT AND HIT A STRONG SHOT. THEREFORE, WE NEED TO ROTATE SHOULDERS TO THE LEFT (RIGHT FOR LEFTIES), TAKE THE RACKET BACK, KEEP ELBOWS AWAY FROM TOUCHING YOUR BODY, SHOULDERS SLIGHTLY FORWARD. FEET, KNEES AND HIPS ARE ALSO LOOKING TO THE LEFT SIDE (RIGHT SIDE FOR LEFTIES).

NOW, IN THIS POSITION MAKE A STEP TOWARDS THE NET (HEEL FIRST) WITH YOUR RIGHT FOOT (LEFT FOOT FOR LEFTIES) AND HIT THE BALL.

FOLLOW THROUGH. WITH THE RACKET TO THE RIGHT SHOULDER. DON'T STOP THE RACKET AFTER YOU HIT THE BALL. THE SHOT ENDS WITH A FOLLOW THROUGH TO THE OPPOSITE SHOULDER. GET BACK IN A READY POSITION.

*NOTE. WE USE A CLOSED STANCE FOR BEGINNERS.

VOLLEY

VOLLEY IS CONSIDERED TO BE AN AGGRESSIVE STROKE. VOLLEYS ARE HIT BEFORE THE BALL BOUNCES OFF THE COURT. USUALLY IT IS AT THE NET BUT CAN ALSO BE HIT FROM THE MIDDLE OF THE COURT. VOLLEYS ARE USED TO WIN POINTS FAST AND TAKE AN OPPONENT BY SURPRISE. A PLAYER'S REACTION TIME SHOULD BE FAST, MOVEMENTS SHORT AND PRECISE. IT REQUIRES HIGH LEVEL OF SKILL, PRECISION, REACTION AND REFLEXES.

VOLLEY IS CONSIDERED TO BE ONE OF THE MORE DIFFICULT STROKES NOT SO MUCH BECAUSE OF THE TECHNIQUE BUT MORE SO BECAUSE OF THE SPEED OF THE BALL. TO HIT A VOLLEY A PLAYER HAS TO MAKE A SERIES OF FAST DECISIONS IN HIS OR HER HEAD AS THE BALL IS HEADED EITHER FOR THEIR FACE OR FAR AWAY FROM THE PLAYER.

THERE ARE DIFFERENT TYPES OF VOLLEYS THAT CAN BE USED IN DIFFERENT SITUATIONS BUT AS BEGINNERS WE ARE GOING TO FOCUS ON THE BLOCK VOLLEY.

TO EXECUTE A VOLLEY, START WITH SOFT LEGS, KNEES BENT, FEET SHOULDER WIDTH APART AND HEELS OFF THE COURT. HOLD A RACKET WITH A CONTINENTAL GRIP.

NOTE.
YOU DON'T WANT TO HIT THE BALL HEAD ON. YOU SHOULD ALWAYS HIT A BALL ON EITHER SIDE OF YOUR BODY AND SLIGHTLY IN FRONT OF YOU.

AS THE BALL IS HEADED TO YOUR SIDE OF THE COURT, ROTATE YOUR SHOULDERS IN THE DIRECTION THAT THE BALL IS TRAVELING TO, BRING YOUR RACKET UP TO THE SIDE OF YOUR BODY, STEP TOWARDS THE NET WITH THE OPPOSITE FOOT (FOR EXAMPLE, IF YOU HIT A VOLLEY ON YOUR RIGHT, USE A LEFT FOOT TO STEP TOWARDS THE NET) AND HIT A BALL.

NOTE.
AT THE POINT OF CONTACT, SQUEEZE THE RACKET TIGHT IN YOUR HAND AND FREEZE FOR A SPLIT SECOND.

DON'T MOVE YOUR ARM FROM TOP TO BOTTOM BUT RATHER FROM TOP, SLIGHTLY TO THE BOTTOM AND FORWARD.

SEQUENCE.
ROTATE SHOULDERS AND MAKE A SWING - STEP TOWARDS THE NET - HIT THE BALL - MOVE THE RACKET DOWN AND FORWARD.

NOTE.
TO HIT A BACKHAND VOLLEY, WE USE DOMINANT HAND AND SLIGHTLY SUPPORT IT WITH THE OTHER HAND.

ROTATE FEET AND SHOULDERS TO THE LEFT, MAKE A SHORT SWING, THE RACKET SHOULD NOT BE TAKEN PAST THE SHOULDERS. ELBOWS SLIGHTLY BENT BUT ARE NOT TOUCHING A PLAYER'S STOMACH AREA. STEP WITH RIGHT FOOT TOWARDS THE NET. REMEMBER TO KEEP KNEES SOFT. HIT THE BALL FROM TOP TO BOTTOM AND EXTEND IT FORWARD.

THERE YOU HAVE IT. KEEP PRACTICING AND YOU'LL MAKE IT PERFECT.

NOTES: ....
....
....
....
....
....
....

IMPORTANT POINTS TO KEEP IN MIND.

- KEEP KNEES SOFT AND BENT.
- SHOULDERS SLIGHTLY FORWARD.
- ELBOWS AWAY FROM THE BODY, ELBOWS SHOULD BE ALMOST STRAIGHT.
- BREATH OUT AS YOU HIT A BALL.
- WHEN PREPARING FOR A SHOT STEP FORWARD TOWARDS THE BALL WITH A HEEL FIRST AND THEN THE REST OF THE FOOT.

SERVICE

SERVICE CAN BE A GREAT ASSET TO YOUR GAME. IT CAN WIN YOU "FREE" POINTS WITH ACES. IT CAN ALSO BE A LIABILITY AND HAVE YOU LOSE A MATCH. IT IS VERY IMPORTANT TO MASTER THIS STROKE AS IT IS THE MOST IMPORTANT ONE IN TENNIS. WITHOUT IT YOU CANNOT PLAY THE GAME. HERE'S A STEP-BY-STEP GUIDE ON HOW TO LEARN TO SERVE.

SWING.

STAND AT THE BASELINE, SLIGHTLY OFF CENTER. IT IS BEST TO START ON AN ADVANTAGE SIDE AS IT IS MORE STRAIGHTFORWARD AND REQUIRES LESS MANIPULATIONS WITH THE BALL TOSS.

RIGHT-HANDED PLAYERS, PUT YOUR LEFT (FRONT) FOOT TO THE LINE (NOT ON THE LINE) IN A WAY THAT IT SHOULD POINT AT THE RIGHT NET POST. RIGHT FOOT IS BEHIND, PARALLEL TO THE BASELINE.

LEFTIES, YOU SHOULD PUT YOUR RIGHT FOOT TO THE LINE (NOT ON THE LINE) IN A WAY THAT IT SHOULD POINT AT THE LEFT NET POST. LEFT FOOT IS BEHIND, PARALLEL TO THE BASELINE.

GRIP. CONTINENTAL GRIP IS THE BEST FOR THIS STROKE. SEE PAGE 31 ON HOW TO HOLD A RACKET WITH A CONTINENTAL GRIP.

BALL TOSS. THIS IS A TRICKY ONE. WHEN TOSSING THE BALL, THE GOAL IS FOR THE BALL TO NOT SPIN IN ANY DIRECTION WHILE IT'S IN THE AIR. IT'S IMPORTANT BECAUSE A PLAYER SHOULD PUT A SPIN ON IT OR SLICE IT WHEN HITTING. THEREFORE, WHEN TOSSING A BALL:

1. EXTEND YOUR ARM IN THE DIRECTION THAT YOU WANT A BALL TO TRAVEL IN.
2. PUT A BALL EITHER ON YOUR PALM AND HOLD IT ONLY WITH YOUR THUMB;

OR
HOLD A BALL WITH YOUR THUMB, INDEX AND MIDDLE FINGERS.

3. BRING YOUR ARM UP AND RELEASE THE BALL AT EYE LEVEL. CONTINUE TO MOVE YOUR LEFT ARM UP.
4. KEEP YOUR EYES ON THE BALL AT ALL TIMES.

LEGS. BEND YOUR KNEES AND EXTEND IT AS YOU JUMP TO HIT THE BALL AT THE HIGHEST POINT.

TRUNK. AS YOU MAKE A BACKSWING, ROTATE YOUR TRUNK TO THE RIGHT (LEFT FOR LEFTIES). THIS IS A COILING MOVEMENT THAT HELPS TO GATHER ENERGY.

BACKSWING.

BACKSWING IS DONE SIMULTANEOUSLY WITH THE BALL TOSS. IT CAN BE TRICKY TO LEARN AT FIRST BUT DON'T GET DISCOURAGED. YOU CAN DO IT! MOVE YOUR DOMINANT ARM TO THE OTHER SIDE OF YOUR BODY. LOOP THE RACKET UP BEHIND YOUR HEAD AND DROP IT BEHIND YOUR BACK. THIS SHOULD LOOK LIKE A TROPHY POSE.

ONCE THE BALL IS AT THE HIGHEST POINT, BRING THE RACKET UP, PRONATE IT AND HIT THE BALL. LEFT ARM THAT WAS TOSSING A BALL SHOULD BE TUCKED AWAY. PLACE IT UNDER YOUR CHEST AS IF YOU HUG YOURSELF. ONCE YOU HIT THE BALL, DON'T STOP THE RACKET. INSTEAD, KEEP THE MOMENTUM GOING AND FOLLOW THROUGH CROSS BODY DOWN TO YOUR LEFT LEG (RIGHT FOR LEFTIES).

FOOTWORK

FOOTWORK IS THE FOUNDATION OF YOUR GAME. IF YOU CANNOT GET TO THE BALL, YOU CANNOT HIT IT. NO MATTER HOW GOOD YOUR TECHNIQUE IS.

THAT'S WHY WE ARE GOING TO DEDICATE TIME DURING EACH PRACTICE TO FOOTWORK.

BELOW IS A LIST OF EXERCISES THAT YOU CAN CHOOSE FROM. I ENCOURAGE YOU TO TRY ALL OF THEM EVEN IF IT SEEMS TOO DIFFICULT. DO EACH EXERCISE FOR 30 SECONDS, 2-3 SETS.

TO SEE THE DEMONSTRATION OF EXERCISES AND DRILLS, PLEASE SCAN THE QR CODE.

1. START AT THE SERVICE LINE. RUN TO THE NET AND TOUCH IT WITH A RACKET. THEN BACKPEDAL BACK TO THE SERVICE LINE AND RUN TO THE NET AGAIN. CONTINUE THE PATTERN FOR 30 SECONDS. COUNT HOW MANY TIMES YOU TOUCH THE NET. WRITE DOWN YOUR RESULTS.

2. SET UP FIVE (5) CONES A COUPLE OF FEET APART ON A DOUBLES LINE. SET FIVE (5) BALLS ON A RACKET IN THE CENTER OF THE SERVICE LINE (T). A COACH STARTS THE TIMER AND A PLAYER PICKS UP ONE BALL AT A TIME, RUNS AND SETS IT UP ON THE CONE. RETURNS FOR THE NEXT BALL. ONCE ALL FIVE BALLS ARE PLACED ON TOP OF THE CONES, A PLAYER CAN TAKE A THIRTY (30) SECONDS BREAK. AFTER THAT, RUN AND PICK UP ONE BALL AT A TIME AND BRING IT BACK TO THE RACKET IN THE CENTER OF THE SERVICE LINE. RECORD YOUR TIME.

3. SET UP 8 - 10 CONES ALONG A SERVICE OR BASE LINE. HOP OVER IT WITH BOTH FEET TOGETHER. TURN AROUND AND HOP BACK.

4. SET UP 8 - 10 CONES ALONG THE SERVICE OR BASE LINE. STAND SIDEWAYS TO THE CONES. MOVE LATERALLY OVER THE CONES THERE AND BACK.

5. SET UP 8 - 10 CONES. SHUFFLE IN A ZIG ZAG PATTERN BETWEEN THE CONES.

NOTES: . . . .
. . . .
. . . .
. . . .
. . . .
. . . .
. . . .
. . . .
. . . .
. . . .
. . . .

6. SET TWO CONES 3-5 FEET APART FROM EACH OTHER AND SHUFFLE FACING THE NET FROM SIDE TO SIDE IN A NUMBER EIGHT PATTERN.

7. SET TWO CONES 3-5 FEET APART. RUN IN A NUMBER EIGHT PATTERN FORWARD AND BACKWARD AROUND THE CONES.

8. SET UP 8-10 CONES A FEW FEET APART. JUMP AND LAND OVER THE CONE WITH FEET SHOULDER WIDTH APART. JUMP IN BETWEEN THE CONES, BRING THE FEET TOGETHER. CONTINUE THIS PATTERN FOR 30 SECONDS.

9. STARTING AT THE NET. DO TWENTY (20) SECONDS HIGH KNEES AND THEN SPRINT TO THE BASELINE.

10. SET UP 3-5 CONES A COUPLE OF FEET APART. A PLAYER AND A COACH STAND ON OPPOSITE SIDES OF THE CONES. A COACH POINTS AT THE CONE AND A PLAYER HAS TO RUN AND TAP IT WITH HIS/HER FOOT. A PLAYER STARTS FROM A SPLIT STEP POSITION.

11. START AT THE CENTER OF THE SERVICE LINE. SHUFFLE TO THE SINGLES SIDE LINE AND BACK TO THE CENTER LINE. COUNT HOW MANY TIMES YOU TAPPED THE LINES.

THESE ARE SOME OF THE BASIC BEGINNER FOOTWORK DRILLS. ONCE YOU MASTER THESE, YOU CAN MOVE TO THE MORE ADVANCED ONES.

NOTES: . . . .
. . . .
. . . .
. . . .
. . . .
. . . .
. . . .
. . . .
. . . .
. . . .
. . . .
. . . .
. . . .
. . . .
. . . .
. . . .
. . . .
. . . .
. . . .
. . . .
. . . .
. . . .
. . . .

CARDIO

THERE ARE A LOT OF BENEFITS TO INCLUDING CARDIO WORKOUTS IN YOUR TRAINING ROUTINE.

EVERYTHING FROM ENRICHING YOUR BLOOD SYSTEM WITH OXYGEN, TO BOOSTING BRAIN ACTIVITY, STRENGTHENING YOUR HEART AND AVOIDING MANY DISEASES. CARDIO CAN ALSO BE JUST PLAIN FUN.

BELOW I SELECTED A FEW CARDIO EXERCISES THAT PROVIDE EXTRA BENEFITS FOR TENNIS PLAYERS:

RUN
DID YOU KNOW THAT TENNIS PLAYERS RUN ABOUT THREE MILES IN A TWO SET MATCH. TO SUSTAIN THAT AND BE ABLE TO PLAY GOOD DURING THE MATCH, YOU SHOULD INCLUDE RUNNING IN YOUR TRAINING ROUTINE. A COUPLE OF MILES THREE TIMES A WEEK IS A GREAT START. IT WILL HELP TO BUILD STRENGTH AND ENDURANCE.

JUMP ROPE
JUST 15 MINUTES OF CONTINUOUS JUMPING AND YOU GOT YOURSELF A GREAT WORKOUT, JUMP ROPE IMPROVES BALANCE, HAND-EYE COORDINATION, MAKES BOTH SIDES OF THE BRAIN WORK AT THE SAME TIME. JUMPING INCREASES BONE DENSITY AND HELPS PREVENT FOOT AND ANKLE INJURIES THAT ARE COMMON AMONGST ATHLETES.

SPRINTS
A TENNIS FUNDAMENTAL. IN ORDER TO GET TO THE BALL, PLAYERS SPRINT FROM THE BASELINE TO THE NET. PRACTICE SPRINTING DURING YOUR CLASSES ALONG THE SIDELINE AND JOG BACK.

THESE ARE THE THREE NECESSARY CARDIO EXERCISES FOR EVERY TENNIS PLAYER. HOWEVER, THERE ARE SO MANY OTHER ACTIVITIES THAT YOU CAN DO TOGETHER AS A FAMILY. FOR EXAMPLE, RIDING BIKES, HIKING, ROLLER SKATING... THE LIST GOES ON. THE IDEA IS TO RAISE YOUR HEART RATE AND TO HAVE FUN.

NOTES: . . . .

SPIDER RUN

1. A PLAYER STARTS IN THE MIDDLE OF THE COURT, IN THE CENTER OF THE SERVICE LINE. A COACH STARTS THE TIMER.

2. A PLAYER RUNS DIAGONALLY TO THE NET AND THE SINGLES LINE CROSSING, TOUCH THE NET. RETURN TO THE CENTER.

3. RUN TO THE OTHER SIDE, TOUCH THE NET. RETURN TO THE CENTER.

4. SHUFFLE SIDEWAYS TO THE SINGLES LINE ALONG THE SERVICE LINE. RETURN TO THE CENTER.

5. SHUFFLE SIDEWAYS TO THE OTHER SIDE. RETURN TO THE CENTER.

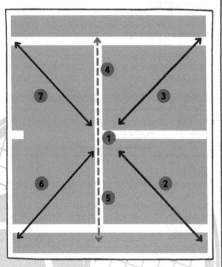

6. RUN DIAGONALLY TO THE BASELINE AND SINGLES LINE CORNER. RETURN TO THE CENTER.

7. RUN TO THE OTHER SIDE. RETURN TO THE CENTER.

RECORD YOUR RESULTS.

RUN THE LINES

A PLAYER STARTS AT THE SERVICE LINE (ON A T). A COACH CALLS A LINE AND A PLAYER HAS TO RUN THERE AND COME BACK TO THE ORIGINAL SPOT. SHOULD RUN TO THE SERVICE LINE AND RETURN TO THE ORIGINAL SPOT. CONTINUE TO SWITCH UP THE DIRECTIONS AND CALL THE LINES FOR 30 SECONDS OR SO.
THIS EXERCISE IS GREAT AS AN EXPRESS WARM UP AND TO LEARN ALL THE LINES ON THE TENNIS COURT FAST.

NOTES: ....
....
....
....
....
....
....
....
....
....
....
....
....
....

TO SEE THE DEMONSTRATION OF EXERCISES AND DRILLS, PLEASE SCAN THE QR CODE.

SPLIT STEP

WHAT IS A SPLIT STEP. A SPLIT STEP IS A VERY BASIC SMALL JUMP WITH BOTH FEET THAT PLAYERS DO BEFORE GOING AFTER THE BALL. IT HELPS PLAYERS TO GAIN BALANCE AND PREPARE FOR THE NEXT SHOT.

TECHNIQUE.

START BY STANDING WITH YOUR FEET SHOULDER WIDTH APART. FEET FACE FORWARD TOWARDS THE NET. KNEES BENT, HEELS OFF THE COURT, ALL THE BODY WEIGHT IS ON THE BALLS OF THE FEET. KEEP SHOULDERS LEANING SLIGHTLY FORWARD. A PLAYER SHOULD JUMP AS THE OPPONENT HITS THE BALL. THIS WAY YOU CAN MAKE IT TO THE BALL IN TIME.

NOTES: ....
....
....
....
....
....
....
....
....
....
....
....
....
....
....
....
....
....
....

HOW TO FEED THE BALLS

WHAT IS FEEDING THE BALLS?
FEEDING THE BALLS IS AN EXPRESSION USED BY TENNIS PLAYERS AND COACHES THAT MEANS TO SIMPLY GET THE BALL INTO THE GAME OR GIVE BALLS TO THE PLAYER TO PRACTICE A CERTAIN STROKE.

HOW TO FEED THE BALLS?
THERE ARE TWO WAYS TO FEED THE BALLS.

HAND-FEEDING

USUALLY USED TO TEACH BEGINNER PLAYERS OR SPEED-HITTING. THAT'S WHEN A COACH STANDS RELATIVELY CLOSE TO A PLAYER AND UNDERHAND TOSSES THE BALLS.

USING A RACKET TO FEED

WHEN A COACH FEEDS THE BALLS FROM THE OTHER SIDE OF THE NET. USING CONTINENTAL GRIP, TOSS A BALL UP IN THE AIR AND HIT IT AS THE BALL TRAVELS DOWN TO YOUR WAIST LEVEL (THE BALL SHOULD NOT BOUNCE OFF THE COURT). HIT IT IN A WAY THAT THERE'S NO SPIN ON THE BALL.

NOTES: ....
....
....
....
....
....
....
....
....
....
....
....
....
....
....

TO SEE THE DEMONSTRATION OF EXERCISES AND DRILLS, PLEASE SCAN THE QR CODE.

LESSON 1

ITEMS NEEDED:
- [ ] RACKET
- [ ] BALLS
- [ ] CONES
- [ ] SPOT MARKERS
- [ ] TENNIS SHOES

OPTIONAL:
- [ ] JUMP ROPE

DATE: __ / __ / __

WARM UP.
- JOG 3-5 LAPS AROUND THE COURT.

DO AT LEAST EIGHT (8) WARM UP EXERCISES FROM PAGE 35 - 36, WRITE IT DOWN.

EXERCISE	REPS/MINS/SECS	EXERCISE	REPS/MINS/SECS
....	....	....	....
....	....	....	....
....	....	....	....
....	....	....	....
....	....	....	....

STRETCH.
DO AT LEAST THREE (3) STRETCHING EXERCISES FROM PAGE 37, WRITE IT DOWN.

EXERCISE	REPS/MINS/SECS	EXERCISE	REPS/MINS/SECS
....	....	....	....
....	....	....	....
....	....	....	....

HAND - EYE COORDINATION.
THE GAME OF TENNIS REQUIRES GREAT HAND-EYE COORDINATION. TENNIS PLAYERS WORK ON IT ALL THROUGHOUT THEIR TENNIS CAREERS. INDEED, IT'S IMPORTANT RIGHT NOW, AS YOU BEGIN YOUR TENNIS JOURNEY.

DO AT LEAST TWO (2) EXERCISES FROM THE LIST ON PAGE 26 - 27, RECORD IT.

EXERCISE	REPS/MINS/SECS	EXERCISE	REPS/MINS/SECS
....	....	....	....
....	....	....	....

REACTION TIME.
ANOTHER IMPORTANT SKILL TO HAVE IS A FAST REACTION TIME. DO AT LEAST TWO (2) EXERCISES FROM THE LIST ON PAGE 24 -25, WRITE IT DOWN.

EXERCISE	REPS/MINS/SECS	EXERCISE	REPS/MINS/SECS
....	....	....	....
....	....	....	....
....	....	....	....

RUN THE LINES.
SEE DESCRIPTION OF THIS EXERCISE ON PAGE 48.

....

LESSON 1

FOREHAND.
THE FIRST STROKE I WOULD LIKE FOR YOU TO LEARN IS A FOREHAND. IT IS PROBABLY THE EASIEST STROKE IN TENNIS. IT CAN ALSO BECOME ONE OF YOUR STRONGEST WEAPONS. SEE TECHNIQUE DESCRIPTION ON PAGE 38 - 39.

STARTING AT THE CENTER OF THE SERVICE LINE, A PLAYER GETS IN A CLOSED STANCE POSITION, MAKES A SWING. A COACH STANDS NEAR A PLAYER AND FEEDS HIM OR HER EASY BALLS (SEE HOW TO PROPERLY TOSS AND FEED THE BALLS ON PAGE 49). THE GOAL IS TO HIT TWENTY FIVE (25) BALLS OVER THE NET AND INTO THE COURT. WE DO NOT COUNT THE BALLS THAT WENT OUT OR INTO THE NET.

NOTE.
A PLAYER IS NOT GOING TO HIT EVERY BALL THE FIRST TIME, IT'S NORMAL. GET YOURSELF A BASKET OF 100-150 BALLS AND BE PATIENT. TOSS THE BALLS EASILY. THE GOAL IS TO HIT 25 BALLS OVER THE NET BY THE END OF THE FIRST PRACTICE. YOU MAY HAVE TO USE TWO OR THREE BASKETS OF BALLS TO GET THERE.

RUN ONE LAP AROUND THE COURT AS FAST AS POSSIBLE ON TIME. A PARENT/COACH START A TIMER. RECORD YOUR RESULTS: . . . .
. . . .

GAME LOBSTER TAIL.
A PLAYER HOLDS A RACKET, A COACH HOLDS A BALL. STAND THREE TO FIVE FEET AWAY FROM EACH OTHER. A COACH EASILY TOSSES A BALL TO THE PLAYER, A PLAYER'S JOB IS TO CATCH A BALL BETWEEN HIS HAND AND A RACKET. TRY TO CATCH SIX (6) BALLS. . . . .
. . . .

FOOTWORK.
FOOTWORK IS ONE OF THE CORNERSTONES TO BECOMING A SUCCESSFUL TENNIS PLAYER. YOU SHOULD DEDICATE EXTRA ATTENTION TO IT. DO AT LEAST THREE(3) EXERCISES FROM PAGE 45 - 46, WRITE IT DOWN.

EXERCISE	REPS/MINS/SECS	EXERCISE	REPS/MINS/SECS
. . . .	. . . .	. . . .	. . . .
. . . .	. . . .	. . . .	. . . .
. . . .	. . . .	. . . .	. . . .

COOL DOWN.
SLOWLY JOG ONE LAP AROUND THE COURT. . . . .

STRETCH.
TO FINISH OFF THE PRACTICE WE NEED TO STRETCH. THIS WILL HELP TO KEEP MUSCLES FROM GETTING TOO SORE. . . . .

LESSON 1

PRACTICE SUMMARY

WHAT I NEED TO WORK ON? . . . .
. . . .
. . . .
. . . .
. . . .
. . . .
. . . .
. . . .
. . . .

COACH'S NOTES: . . . .
. . . .
. . . .
. . . .
. . . .
. . . .
. . . .
. . . .

WHAT DID I DO GOOD TODAY? . . . .
. . . .
. . . .
. . . .
. . . .
. . . .
. . . .

MY NOTES: . . . .
. . . .
. . . .
. . . .
. . . .
. . . .
. . . .
. . . .

IMPORTANT POINTS TO REMEMBER:

- KEEP KNEES BENT.
- KEEP HEELS OFF THE COURT.
- WHEN MAKING A SWING AND HITTING A BALL ELBOWS SHOULD NOT TOUCH A PLAYER'S STOMACH AREA.
- KEEP ELBOWS SLIGHTLY BENT (ALMOST STRAIGHT).
- DON'T FORGET TO FOLLOW THROUGH AFTER CONTACT WITH THE BALL.

RATE LESSON:

☆ ☆ ☆ ☆ ☆

GREAT JOB TODAY!
KEEP IT UP!

LESSON 2

ITEMS NEEDED:
- [ ] RACKET
- [ ] BALLS
- [ ] CONES
- [ ] SPOT MARKERS
- [ ] TENNIS SHOES

OPTIONAL:
- [ ] JUMP ROPE

DATE: __ / __ / __

☹ 🙁 😐 🙂 😎

WARM UP.
- JOG 3-5 LAPS AROUND THE COURT.

DO AT LEAST EIGHT (8) WARM UP EXERCISES FROM PAGE 35 - 36, WRITE IT DOWN.

EXERCISE	REPS/MINS/SECS	EXERCISE	REPS/MINS/SECS
....		....	
....		....	
....		....	
....		....	
....		....	

STRETCH.
DO AT LEAST THREE (3) STRETCHING EXERCISES FROM PAGE 37, WRITE IT DOWN.

EXERCISE	REPS/MINS/SECS	EXERCISE	REPS/MINS/SECS
....		....	
....		....	
....		....	

HAND - EYE COORDINATION.
THE GAME OF TENNIS REQUIRES GREAT HAND-EYE COORDINATION. TENNIS PLAYERS WORK ON IT ALL THROUGHOUT THEIR TENNIS CAREERS. INDEED, IT'S IMPORTANT RIGHT NOW, AS YOU BEGIN YOUR TENNIS JOURNEY.

DO AT LEAST TWO (2) EXERCISES FROM THE LIST ON PAGE 26 - 27, RECORD IT.

EXERCISE	REPS/MINS/SECS	EXERCISE	REPS/MINS/SECS
....		....	
....		....	

REACTION TIME.
ANOTHER IMPORTANT SKILL TO HAVE IS A FAST REACTION TIME. DO AT LEAST TWO (2) EXERCISES FROM THE LIST ON PAGE 24 -25, WRITE IT DOWN.

EXERCISE	REPS/MINS/SECS	EXERCISE	REPS/MINS/SECS
....		....	
....		....	
....		....	

STROKE PRODUCTION. FOREHAND.
STARTING AT THE CENTER OF THE SERVICE LINE, REVIEW THE FOREHAND. HAVE A PLAYER STAND SIDEWAYS TO THE NET, LEFT ARM (FOR RIGHT HAND DOMINANT PLAYERS) POINTING AT THE BALL.

A PARENT/COACH STANDS NEAR AND TOSSES EASY BALLS TO HIM OR HER. LET THE PLAYER GAIN CONFIDENCE, THAT HE CAN ACTUALLY HIT THE BALL. HIT ANYWHERE BETWEEN 20-30 BALLS OVER THE NET AND INTO THE COURT.

RUN ONE LAP AROUND THE COURT AS FAST AS POSSIBLE ON TIME. A PARENT/COACH START A TIMER. RECORD YOUR RESULTS: . . . .

ONCE A PLAYER START TO FEEL MORE CONFIDENT HITTING BALLS FROM ONE SPOT, TEACH HIM OR HER TO MOVE TO THE BALL AND HIT IT, BY ADDING A LITTLE DISTANCE. A PARENT/COACH CONTINUES TO STAND NEAR A PLAYER BUT AT A DISTANCE SO THAT NOBODY GETS HIT WITH A RACKET.

DRILL 1.
TOSS A BALL SLIGHTLY TO THE SIDE, WHERE A PLAYER HAS TO MAKE TWO-THREE SMALL STEPS, GET IN A READY POSITION AND HIT THE BALL. SHUFFLE BACK TO THE CENTER. HIT 20-30 BALLS OVER THE NET AND INTO THE COURT.

FOOTWORK.
LET A PLAYER STAND IN BETWEEN THE SINGLES SIDE LINE AND THE CENTER LINE OF THE SERVICE BOX. A PLAYER SHOULD SHUFFLE SIDEWAYS BETWEEN TWO LINES AS FAST AS POSSIBLE FOR 30 SECONDS. COUNT HOW MANY TIMES HE OR SHE TAPS EACH LINE. RECORD YOUR RESULTS. . . . .
. . . .

DRILL 2.
NEXT DRILL IS ALSO FOCUSED ON THE FOREHAND. THIS TIME PUT A CONE IN THE MIDDLE OF THE SERVICE LINE (ON A T). A PLAYER HAS TO HIT THE BALL AND SHUFFLE AROUND THE CONE. THE GOAL IS TO HIT ANOTHER 25-30 BALLS INTO THE OPPOSITE SIDE OF THE COURT.

NOTE.
WHILE SHUFFLING, A PLAYER SHOULD HAVE HIS SHOULDERS SQUARED TO THE NET. IN OTHER WORDS, SHOULDERS SHOULD "LOOK" AT THE NET.
AGAIN, IT MAY TAKE ONE BASKET OF BALLS TO ACHIEVE THIS GOAL, IT MAY TAKE THREE. DO NOT RUSH AND ENCOURAGE YOUR CHILD TO HIT MORE AND TRY HARDER.

GAME. LOBSTER TAIL - ADVANCED.
A PLAYER HOLDS TWO RACKETS, ONE IN EACH HAND; A COACH HOLDS A BALL. STAND THREE TO FIVE FEET AWAY FROM EACH OTHER. A COACH EASILY TOSSES A BALL TO THE PLAYER, A PLAYER'S JOB IS TO CATCH A BALL WITH BOTH RACKETS. DO NOT TOUCH THE BALL WITH HANDS. TRY TO CATCH EIGHT (8) BALLS.

TIP.
A PARENT/COACH CAN MAKE IT SLIGHTLY UNPREDICTABLE AND TOSS THE BALLS IN DIFFERENT DIRECTIONS SLIGHTLY AWAY FROM THE PLAYER.

LESSON 2

COOL DOWN.
SLOWLY JOG ONE LAP AROUND THE COURT.....................................

STRETCH.
TO FINISH OFF THE PRACTICE WE NEED TO STRETCH. THIS WILL HELP TO KEEP
MUSCLES FROM GETTING TOO SORE.....................................

PRACTICE SUMMARY
WHAT I NEED TO WORK ON?.....................................
....
....
....
....
....

COACH'S NOTES:.....................................
....
....
....
....
....
....

WHAT DID I DO GOOD TODAY?.....................................
....
....
....
....
....

MY NOTES:.....................................
....
....
....
....
....
....

IMPORTANT POINTS TO REMEMBER:
- KEEP KNEES BENT.
- KEEP HEELS OFF THE COURT.
- WHEN MAKING A SWING AND HITTING A BALL ELBOWS SHOULD NOT TOUCH A PLAYER'S STOMACH AREA.
- KEEP ELBOWS SLIGHTLY BENT (ALMOST STRAIGHT).
- DON'T FORGET TO FOLLOW THROUGH AFTER CONTACT WITH THE BALL.

RATE LESSON:

☆☆☆☆☆

**GREAT JOB TODAY!
KEEP IT UP!**

LESSON 3

ITEMS NEEDED:

- [ ] RACKET
- [ ] BALLS
- [ ] CONES
- [ ] SPOT MARKERS
- [ ] TENNIS SHOES

OPTIONAL:

- [ ] JUMP ROPE

DATE: __ / __ / __

☹ 😐 😄 😊 😤

WARM UP.

- JOG 3-5 LAPS AROUND THE COURT.

DO AT LEAST EIGHT (8) WARM UP EXERCISES FROM PAGE 35 - 36, WRITE IT DOWN.

EXERCISE	REPS/MINS/SECS	EXERCISE	REPS/MINS/SECS
....	....	....	....
....	....	....	....
....	....	....	....
....	....	....	....
....	....	....	....

STRETCH.

DO AT LEAST THREE (3) STRETCHING EXERCISES FROM PAGE 37, WRITE IT DOWN.

EXERCISE	REPS/MINS/SECS	EXERCISE	REPS/MINS/SECS
....	....	....	....
....	....	....	....
....	....	....	....

HAND - EYE COORDINATION.

THE GAME OF TENNIS REQUIRES GREAT HAND-EYE COORDINATION. TENNIS PLAYERS WORK ON IT ALL THROUGHOUT THEIR TENNIS CAREERS. INDEED, IT'S IMPORTANT RIGHT NOW, AS YOU BEGIN YOUR TENNIS JOURNEY.

DO AT LEAST TWO (2) EXERCISES FROM THE LIST ON PAGE 26 - 27, RECORD IT.

EXERCISE	REPS/MINS/SECS	EXERCISE	REPS/MINS/SECS
....	....	....	....
....	....	....	....

REACTION TIME.

ANOTHER IMPORTANT SKILL TO HAVE IS A FAST REACTION TIME. DO AT LEAST TWO (2) EXERCISES FROM THE LIST ON PAGE 24 -25, WRITE IT DOWN.

EXERCISE	REPS/MINS/SECS	EXERCISE	REPS/MINS/SECS
....	....	....	....
....	....	....	....
....	....	....	....

STROKE PRODUCTION. BACKHAND.

BEFORE WE BEGIN, I WOULD LIKE TO REMIND THAT A COACH/PARENT SHOULD FEED THE BALLS EASILY AND STAND RELATIVELY CLOSE TO A PLAYER, ON THE SAME SIDE OF THE COURT.

START BY HOLDING A RACKET WITH A NON-DOMINANT HAND ONLY, TURN SIDEWAYS TO THE NET AND HIT 20-30 BALLS OVER THE NET. START AT THE CENTER OF THE SERVICE LINE. KEEP YOUR LEFT ARM ALMOST STRAIGHT AND AWAY FROM THE BODY (ELBOWS SHOULD NOT TOUCH THE STOMACH AREA), KNEES BENT.

THIS EXERCISE IS MEANT FOR A PLAYER TO LEARN THE FEELING OF A LEFT HAND HITTING THE BALLS AND THE STRENGTH THAT SHE/HE SHOULD USE WHEN HITTING A BALL.

NEXT UP, HOLD THE RACKET WITH BOTH HANDS. FOR GRIP INFORMATION SEE PAGE 28, 34.

STARTING AT THE CENTER OF THE SERVICE LINE, KNEES SOFT AND BENT, MAKE A SWING AND HIT 30-50 BALLS WITH TWO-HANDED BACKHAND. . . . .
. . . .

RUN ONE LAP AROUND THE COURT AS FAST AS POSSIBLE ON TIME. A PARENT/COACH START A TIMER. RECORD YOUR RESULTS: . . . .

ONCE THE PLAYER START TO FEEL CONFIDENT HITTING THE BALLS FROM ONE SPOT IN A STANDING POSITION, START TOSSING BALLS SLIGHTLY TO THE SIDE. ENCOURAGE A PLAYER TO MAKE TWO - THREE SMALL STEPS TO GET TO THE BALL.

NOTE.
THIS MAY SEEM LIKE A DIFFICULT STROKE TO MASTER AT FIRST, BUT WITH SOME DEDICATION AND PRACTICE, BACKHAND MAY BECOME YOUR STRONGEST WEAPON.

NOW LET'S REVIEW WHAT WE'VE LEARNED IN THE PREVIOUS CLASS.
HIT 50 FOREHAND STROKES FROM THE SERVICE LINE: START SLOW AND HIT 25-30 BALLS FROM STANDING POSITION.
THEN GRADUALLY ADD THE DISTANCE, SO THAT A PLAYER CAN RUN A FEW STEPS TO GET TO THE BALL. . . . .
. . . .
. . . .

GAME.
SET THE RACKET DOWN ON A BASELINE. SET 5 (FIVE) BALLS ON A RACKET. A PARENT (COACH) STARTS THE TIMER AND A PLAYER SHOULD TAKE THE BALLS ONE AT A TIME TO THE POINTS WHERE COURT LINES MEET OR INTERSECT. SEE THE PICTURE. . . . .
. . . .
. . . .
. . . .
. . . .

LESSON 3

COOL DOWN.
SLOWLY JOG ONE LAP AROUND THE COURT. . . . .

STRETCH.
TO FINISH OFF THE PRACTICE WE NEED TO STRETCH. THIS WILL HELP TO KEEP
MUSCLES FROM GETTING TOO SORE. . . . .

PRACTICE SUMMARY
WHAT I NEED TO WORK ON? . . . .
. . . .
. . . .
. . . .
. . . .
. . . .

COACH'S NOTES: . . . .
. . . .
. . . .
. . . .
. . . .
. . . .

WHAT DID I DO GOOD TODAY? . . . .
. . . .
. . . .
. . . .
. . . .
. . . .

MY NOTES: . . . .
. . . .
. . . .
. . . .
. . . .
. . . .

IMPORTANT POINTS TO REMEMBER:
- KEEP KNEES BENT.
- KEEP HEELS OFF THE COURT.
- WHEN MAKING A SWING AND HITTING A BALL ELBOWS SHOULD NOT TOUCH A PLAYER'S STOMACH AREA.
- KEEP ELBOWS SLIGHTLY BENT (ALMOST STRAIGHT).
- DON'T FORGET TO FOLLOW THROUGH AFTER CONTACT WITH THE BALL.

RATE LESSON:
☆ ☆ ☆ ☆ ☆

GREAT JOB TODAY! KEEP IT UP!

LESSON 4

ITEMS NEEDED:

☐ RACKET ☐ SPOT MARKERS
☐ BALLS ☐ TENNIS SHOES
☐ CONES

OPTIONAL:

☐ JUMP ROPE

DATE: __ / __ / __

☺☺☺☺☺

WARM UP.

• JOG 3-5 LAPS AROUND THE COURT.

DO AT LEAST EIGHT (8) WARM UP EXERCISES FROM PAGE 35 - 36, WRITE IT DOWN.

EXERCISE	REPS/MINS/SECS	EXERCISE	REPS/MINS/SECS
....	....	....	....
....	....	....	....
....	....	....	....
....	....	....	....

STRETCH.

DO AT LEAST THREE (3) STRETCHING EXERCISES FROM PAGE 37, WRITE IT DOWN.

EXERCISE	REPS/MINS/SECS	EXERCISE	REPS/MINS/SECS
....	....	....	....
....	....	....	....
....	....	....	....

REACTION TIME.

ANOTHER IMPORTANT SKILL TO HAVE IS A FAST REACTION TIME. DO AT LEAST TWO (2) EXERCISES FROM THE LIST ON PAGE 24 -25, WRITE IT DOWN.

EXERCISE	REPS/MINS/SECS	EXERCISE	REPS/MINS/SECS
....	....	....	....
....	....	....	....
....	....	....	....

TWO-HANDED BACKHAND.
REVIEW. DRILL 1.

START IN THE MIDDLE OF THE SERVICE LINE, HIT 25-30 BALLS OVER THE NET AND INTO THE COURT. . . . .

RUN ONE LAP AROUND THE COURT AS FAST AS POSSIBLE ON TIME. A PARENT/COACH START A TIMER. RECORD YOUR RESULTS: . . . .

DRILL 2.

HIT A BACKHAND AND RUN A FEW SMALL STEPS TO THE BALL. AGAIN, START AT THE CENTER OF THE SERVICE LINE. HIT ABOUT 25-30 BALLS. . . . .
YOU ARE DOING AMAZING!

NOTE.
I RECOMMEND TO STICK WITH THE SERVICE LINE UNTIL A PLAYER LEARNS TO CONTROL THE BALL SOMEWHAT AND CAN RALLY ON A HALF COURT.

A COACH SHOULD FEED THE BALLS EASILY AND FROM A CLOSE DISTANCE.

FOOTWORK.
SHUFFLE FROM SIDE TO SIDE BETWEEN THE SINGLES SIDELINE AND THE CENTER LINE OF THE SERVICE BOX. SET 30 SECONDS ON TIMER AND GO! COUNT EVERY TIME YOU TAP EACH LINE. WRITE DOWN YOUR RESULTS AND SEE HOW YOU IMPROVE OVER THE NEXT FEW WEEKS. . . . .
. . . .

FOREHAND.
SAME AS WITH A BACKHAND, STARTING AT THE CENTER OF THE SERVICE LINE, HIT 25-30 BALLS WHILE RUNNING. TOSS THE BALLS SLIGHTLY TO THE SIDE. MAKE A PLAYER RUN. . . . .
FANTASTIC JOB!

COMBINE THE TWO STROKES.
ALTERNATE BETWEEN FOREHAND AND BACKHAND STROKES. AFTER EACH SHOT RETURN TO THE CENTER, DO A SPLIT STEP (SEE PAGE 49 FOR TECHNIQUE) AND RUN TO HIT A BACKHAND. DO 30 REPETITIONS. . . . .
. . . .

GAME. ICE CREAM CONE.
A PLAYER AND A COACH STAND ABOUT FIVE(5) FEET APART. YOU CAN ADJUST THE DISTANCE BASED ON AGE AND ABILITIES.
TAKE A CONE, TURN IT UPSIDE DOWN AND HAVE A PLAYER HOLD IT. A COACH/PARENT TOSSES A BALL AND A PLAYER SHOULD CATCH IT WITH A CONE WITHOUT TOUCHING IT WITH HIS/HER HANDS. TOSS THREE BALLS.

P.S. IF YOU DON'T HAVE CONES, YOU CAN USE A BALL CAN.
. . . .
. . . .
. . . .
. . . .
. . . .

COOL DOWN.
SLOWLY JOG ONE LAP AROUND THE COURT. . . . .

STRETCH.
TO FINISH OFF THE PRACTICE WE NEED TO STRETCH. THIS WILL HELP TO KEEP MUSCLES FROM GETTING TOO SORE. . . . .

LESSON 4

PRACTICE SUMMARY

WHAT I NEED TO WORK ON? . . . .
. . . .
. . . .
. . . .
. . . .
. . . .
. . . .
. . . .

COACH'S NOTES: . . . .
. . . .
. . . .
. . . .
. . . .
. . . .
. . . .

WHAT DID I DO GOOD TODAY? . . . .
. . . .
. . . .
. . . .
. . . .
. . . .
. . . .

MY NOTES: . . . .
. . . .
. . . .
. . . .
. . . .
. . . .
. . . .
. . . .

IMPORTANT POINTS TO REMEMBER:

- KEEP KNEES BENT.
- KEEP HEELS OFF THE COURT.
- WHEN MAKING A SWING AND HITTING A BALL ELBOWS SHOULD NOT TOUCH A PLAYER'S STOMACH AREA.
- KEEP ELBOWS SLIGHTLY BENT (ALMOST STRAIGHT).
- DON'T FORGET TO FOLLOW THROUGH AFTER CONTACT WITH THE BALL.

RATE LESSON:

**GREAT JOB TODAY!
KEEP IT UP!**

LESSON 5

ITEMS NEEDED:

- [ ] RACKET
- [ ] BALLS
- [ ] CONES
- [ ] SPOT MARKERS
- [ ] TENNIS SHOES

OPTIONAL:

- [ ] JUMP ROPE

DATE: __ / __ / __

WARM UP.

- JOG 3-5 LAPS AROUND THE COURT.

DO AT LEAST EIGHT (8) WARM UP EXERCISES FROM PAGE 35 - 36, WRITE IT DOWN.

EXERCISE	REPS/MINS/SECS	EXERCISE	REPS/MINS/SECS
....	....	....	....
....	....	....	....
....	....	....	....
....	....	....	....

STRETCH.

DO AT LEAST THREE (3) STRETCHING EXERCISES FROM PAGE 37, WRITE IT DOWN.

EXERCISE	REPS/MINS/SECS	EXERCISE	REPS/MINS/SECS
....	....	....	....
....	....	....	....

HAND - EYE COORDINATION.

THE GAME OF TENNIS REQUIRES GREAT HAND-EYE COORDINATION. TENNIS PLAYERS WORK ON IT ALL THROUGHOUT THEIR TENNIS CAREERS. INDEED, IT'S IMPORTANT RIGHT NOW, AS YOU BEGIN YOUR TENNIS JOURNEY.

DO AT LEAST TWO (2) EXERCISES FROM THE LIST ON PAGE 26 - 27, RECORD IT.

EXERCISE	REPS/MINS/SECS	EXERCISE	REPS/MINS/SECS
....	....	....	....
....	....	....	....

REACTION TIME.

ANOTHER IMPORTANT SKILL TO HAVE IS A FAST REACTION TIME. DO AT LEAST TWO (2) EXERCISES FROM THE LIST ON PAGE 24 -25, WRITE IT DOWN.

EXERCISE	REPS/MINS/SECS	EXERCISE	REPS/MINS/SECS
....	....	....	....
....	....	....	....

NOTE.

A PARENT/COACH SHOULD STAND CLOSER TO THE NET, ON THE SAME SIDE OF THE COURT AS A PLAYER. FEED EASY BALLS, WITH UNDERHAND TOSS.

LESSON 5

DRILL 1.
ON THE SERVICE LINE, START WITH HITTING 20 FOREHANDS AND 20 BACKHANDS
WHILE MAKING A FEW SMALL AND EASY STEPS TOWARDS THE BALL............
....

DRILL 2.
SET UP THREE SPOT MARKERS ON THE SERVICE LINE. ONE IN THE CENTER, A
COUPLE OF FEET BEHIND THE SERVICE LINE; ONE ON FOREHAND SIDE AND ONE ON
BACKHAND SIDE. IT OFFERS PLAYERS A VISUAL WHERE TO RUN AND WHEN TO
PREPARE FOR A STROKE. TRY TO TOSS BALLS SO THAT A PLAYER CAN HIT IT FROM
THE MARKERS. ALTERNATE BETWEEN FOREHAND AND BACKHAND STROKES. AFTER
EACH SHOT SHUFFLE BEHIND THE MIDDLE SPOT MARKER. REPEAT 30 TIMES.......
....

SPIDER RUN.
SEE DESCRIPTION OF THIS EXERCISE ON PAGE 48.
RECORD YOUR RESULTS..
....

DRILL 3.
SET UP FOUR (4) SPOT MARKERS SLIGHTLY BEHIND THE SERVICE LINE. TWO ON
DEUCE SIDE AND TWO ON ADVANTAGE SIDE.
FIRST, HAVE A PLAYER HIT TWO FOREHAND STROKES. A PARENT/COACH/FRIEND
SHOULD FEED THE BALLS EASY TO THE PLAYER FROM A CLOSE DISTANCE.
NEXT, A PLAYER SHOULD SHUFFLE SIDEWAYS TO THE BACKHAND SIDE AND HIT
TWO BACKHAND STROKES...

NOTE.
A PLAYER SHOULD MOVE IN A SHUFFLE FROM FOREHAND SIDE TO BACKHAND.
REPEAT THE DRILL (ALL FOUR STROKES) AT LEAST 10-15 TIMES.

GAME.
A PLAYER IS BEHIND THE BASELINE. A COACH/PARENT AT THE SERVICE LINE. A
COACH ROLLS BALLS ONE AT A TIME IN DIFFERENT DIRECTIONS AND A PLAYER HAS
TO RUN FAST AND CATCH IT BEFORE IT CROSSES THE LINE. ROLL OR TOSS IT BACK
TO THE COACH...
....

COOL DOWN.
SLOWLY JOG ONE LAP AROUND THE COURT.................................

STRETCH.
TO FINISH OFF THE PRACTICE WE NEED TO STRETCH. THIS WILL HELP TO KEEP
MUSCLES FROM GETTING TOO SORE.....................................

LESSON 5

PRACTICE SUMMARY

WHAT I NEED TO WORK ON? . . . .
. . . .
. . . .
. . . .
. . . .
. . . .
. . . .
. . . .
. . . .

COACH'S NOTES: . . . .
. . . .
. . . .
. . . .
. . . .
. . . .
. . . .
. . . .

WHAT DID I DO GOOD TODAY? . . . .
. . . .
. . . .
. . . .
. . . .
. . . .
. . . .

MY NOTES: . . . .
. . . .
. . . .
. . . .
. . . .
. . . .
. . . .
. . . .

IMPORTANT POINTS TO REMEMBER:

- KEEP KNEES BENT.
- KEEP HEELS OFF THE COURT.
- WHEN MAKING A SWING AND HITTING A BALL ELBOWS SHOULD NOT TOUCH A PLAYER'S STOMACH AREA.
- KEEP ELBOWS SLIGHTLY BENT (ALMOST STRAIGHT).
- DON'T FORGET TO FOLLOW THROUGH AFTER CONTACT WITH THE BALL.

RATE LESSON:

GREAT JOB TODAY! KEEP IT UP!

64

LESSON 6

WARM UP.
- JOG 3-5 LAPS AROUND THE COURT.

DO AT LEAST EIGHT (8) WARM UP EXERCISES FROM PAGE 35 - 36, WRITE IT DOWN.

EXERCISE	REPS/MINS/SECS	EXERCISE	REPS/MINS/SECS
. . . .		. . . .	
. . . .		. . . .	
. . . .		. . . .	
. . . .		. . . .	
. . . .		. . . .	

STRETCH.
DO AT LEAST THREE (3) STRETCHING EXERCISES FROM PAGE 37, WRITE IT DOWN.

EXERCISE	REPS/MINS/SECS	EXERCISE	REPS/MINS/SECS
. . . .		. . . .	
. . . .		. . . .	
. . . .		. . . .	

HAND - EYE COORDINATION.
THE GAME OF TENNIS REQUIRES GREAT HAND-EYE COORDINATION. TENNIS PLAYERS WORK ON IT ALL THROUGHOUT THEIR TENNIS CAREERS. INDEED, IT'S IMPORTANT RIGHT NOW, AS YOU BEGIN YOUR TENNIS JOURNEY.

DO AT LEAST TWO (2) EXERCISES FROM THE LIST ON PAGE 26 - 27, RECORD IT.

EXERCISE	REPS/MINS/SECS	EXERCISE	REPS/MINS/SECS
. . . .		. . . .	
. . . .		. . . .	

REACTION TIME.
ANOTHER IMPORTANT SKILL TO HAVE IS A FAST REACTION TIME. DO AT LEAST TWO (2) EXERCISES FROM THE LIST ON PAGE 24 -25, WRITE IT DOWN.

EXERCISE	REPS/MINS/SECS	EXERCISE	REPS/MINS/SECS
. . . .		. . . .	
. . . .		. . . .	
. . . .		. . . .	

VOLLEY.
TODAY WE ARE GOING TO INTRODUCE A VOLLEY.
VOLLEYS ARE MY FAVORITE SHOTS. IT REQUIRES FAST THINKING AND GREAT REACTION TIME AND IF EXECUTED RIGHT, IT'S ALMOST ALWAYS A WINNING POINT.

STEP 1.
TO START, A PLAYER AND A COACH SHOULD STAND ON OPPOSITE SIDES OF THE NET. A COACH IS GOING TO TOSS A BALL EASILY TO THE PLAYER AND A PLAYER SHOULD CATCH THE BALL WITH HIS/HER HANDS AND TOSS IT EASILY BACK TO THE COACH AND RETURN TO THE CENTER. REPEAT 20-30 TIMES.

NOTE.
START TOSSING CLOSE TO THE PLAYER, SO THAT HE OR SHE GETS THE FEEL OF IT. THEN TRY TO THROW THE BALLS SLIGHTLY TO BOTH SIDES, SO THAT A PLAYER HAS TO RUN TO CATCH IT.

STEP 2.
CONTINUE AT THE NET, A COACH EASILY TOSSES THE BALL CLOSE TO THE PLAYER. A PLAYER SHOULD HIT THE BALL WITH HIS/HER HAND BACK OVER THE NET. REPEAT 20-30 TIMES.

STEP 3.
PICK UP A RACKET. USING A CONTINENTAL GRIP, HIT 20 VOLLEYS ON A FOREHAND SIDE. SWITCH SIDES. HIT 20 VOLLEYS ON A BACKHAND SIDE. FOR TECHNIQUE, SEE PAGE 41 - 42.

RUN ONE LAP AROUND THE COURT AS FAST AS POSSIBLE ON TIME. A PARENT/COACH START A TIMER. RECORD YOUR RESULTS:
....

FOREHAND AND BACKHAND.
START AT THE CENTER OF THE SERVICE LINE. PLACE A SPOT MARKER IN THE MIDDLE. HIT FOREHAND AND BACKHAND STROKES CROSS COURT. AFTER EACH STROKE SHUFFLE BACK TO THE CENTER AND MAKE A SPLIT STEP. REPEAT 30 TIMES.

FOOTWORK.
DO AT LEAST ONE (1) EXERCISE FROM PAGE 45 - 46, WRITE IT DOWN.

EXERCISE	REPS/MINS/SECS	EXERCISE	REPS/MINS/SECS
....		....	
....		....	

DRILL.
SET UP FOUR (4) SPOT MARKERS, TWO ON A FOREHAND SIDE AND TWO ON A BACKHAND SIDE, IN "NO MAN'S LAND". ALTERNATE STROKES BETWEEN FOREHAND AND BACKHAND. DO A SPLIT STEP IN THE CENTER AS YOU PREPARE TO HIT ANOTHER SHOT. A COACH/PARENT SHOULD STILL FEED EASY BALLS FROM A SHORT DISTANCE. THE FOCUS SHOULD CONTINUE TO BE ON A TECHNIQUE AND WE ARE STARTING TO ADD A LITTLE BIT OF A FOOTWORK. REPEAT THIS DRILL (ALL FOUR STROKES) AT LEAST 10-15 TIMES.

GAME.
SET UP A BASKET/ HOOLA HOOP OR JUST A SPOT MARKER ON THE OPPOSITE SIDE OF THE COURT FROM A PLAYER. PREFERABLY BETWEEN A NET AND A SERVICE LINE. TOSS EASY BALLS TO THE PLAYER AND HE/SHE SHOULD HIT IT IN A WAY THAT THE BALLS END UP EITHER IN THE BASKET OR BOUNCE OFF OF THE SPOT MARKER. THE GOAL IS TO HIT AT LEAST 6 BALLS IN.

LESSON 6

COOL DOWN.
SLOWLY JOG ONE LAP AROUND THE COURT. . . . .

STRETCH.
TO FINISH OFF THE PRACTICE WE NEED TO STRETCH. THIS WILL HELP TO KEEP
MUSCLES FROM GETTING TOO SORE. . . . .

PRACTICE SUMMARY
WHAT I NEED TO WORK ON? . . . .
. . . .
. . . .
. . . .
. . . .
. . . .

COACH'S NOTES: . . . .
. . . .
. . . .
. . . .
. . . .
. . . .

WHAT DID I DO GOOD TODAY? . . . .
. . . .
. . . .
. . . .
. . . .
. . . .

MY NOTES: . . . .
. . . .
. . . .
. . . .
. . . .
. . . .

IMPORTANT POINTS TO REMEMBER:
- KEEP KNEES BENT.
- KEEP HEELS OFF THE COURT.
- WHEN MAKING A SWING AND HITTING A BALL ELBOWS
  SHOULD NOT TOUCH A PLAYER'S STOMACH AREA.
- KEEP ELBOWS SLIGHTLY BENT (ALMOST STRAIGHT).
- DON'T FORGET TO FOLLOW THROUGH AFTER CONTACT
  WITH THE BALL.

RATE LESSON:

**GREAT JOB TODAY!
KEEP IT UP!**

LESSON 7

ITEMS NEEDED:

- [ ] RACKET
- [ ] BALLS
- [ ] CONES
- [ ] SPOT MARKERS
- [ ] TENNIS SHOES

OPTIONAL:

- [ ] JUMP ROPE

DATE: __ / __ / __

☹ 😐 😄 😊 😣

WARM UP.

- JOG 3-5 LAPS AROUND THE COURT.

DO AT LEAST EIGHT (8) WARM UP EXERCISES FROM PAGE 35 - 36, WRITE IT DOWN.

EXERCISE	REPS/MINS/SECS	EXERCISE	REPS/MINS/SECS
....	....	....	....
....	....	....	....
....	....	....	....
....	....	....	....
....	....	....	....

STRETCH.

DO AT LEAST THREE (3) STRETCHING EXERCISES FROM PAGE 37, WRITE IT DOWN.

EXERCISE	REPS/MINS/SECS	EXERCISE	REPS/MINS/SECS
....	....	....	....
....	....	....	....
....	....	....	....

HAND - EYE COORDINATION.

THE GAME OF TENNIS REQUIRES GREAT HAND-EYE COORDINATION. TENNIS PLAYERS WORK ON IT ALL THROUGHOUT THEIR TENNIS CAREERS. INDEED, IT'S IMPORTANT RIGHT NOW, AS YOU BEGIN YOUR TENNIS JOURNEY.

DO AT LEAST TWO (2) EXERCISES FROM THE LIST ON PAGE 26 - 27, RECORD IT.

EXERCISE	REPS/MINS/SECS	EXERCISE	REPS/MINS/SECS
....	....	....	....
....	....	....	....

REACTION TIME.

ANOTHER IMPORTANT SKILL TO HAVE IS A FAST REACTION TIME. DO AT LEAST TWO (2) EXERCISES FROM THE LIST ON PAGE 24 -25, WRITE IT DOWN.

EXERCISE	REPS/MINS/SECS	EXERCISE	REPS/MINS/SECS
....	....	....	....
....	....	....	....
....	....	....	....

REVIEW.

START BY HITTING 50 FOREHAND BLOCK VOLLEYS. DON'T TRY TO REACH THE BALL FROM ONE POSITION. IT WILL NOT PRODUCE A QUALITY STROKE. IF THE BALL IS TRAVELING SLIGHTLY TO THE SIDE, A PLAYER SHOULD TAKE A FEW SMALL AND FAST STEPS TO THE BALL.

LESSON 7

HIT 50 BACKHAND BLOCK VOLLEYS:
. . . .

RUN THE LINES ON TIME.
SEE DESCRIPTION OF THIS EXERCISE ON PAGE 48. RECORD YOUR RESULTS:
. . . .

GROUND STROKES. DRILL 1.
START ON THE SERVICE LINE BY ALTERNATING FOREHAND AND BACKHAND STROKES. A COACH/PARENT/PARTNER FEEDS THE BALLS GENTLY. A PLAYER STARTS WITH A SPLIT STEP. AT THIS STAGE, A BALL SHOULD BOUNCE NO FURTHER THAN THREE SMALL STEPS AWAY FROM THE CENTER OF THE SERVICE LINE. THIS WILL HELP A PLAYER TO START DEVELOPING SOME RHYTHM. AFTER EACH SHOT RETURN TO THE CENTER AND DO A SPLIT STEP. REPEAT 30-50 TIMES.

RUN ONE LAP AROUND THE COURT AS FAST AS POSSIBLE ON TIME. A PARENT/COACH START A TIMER. RECORD YOUR RESULTS: . . . .
. . . .

GROUND STROKES. DRILL 2.
SET UP SIX (6) SPOT MARKERS A FEW FEET APART FROM THE SERVICE LINE DOWN TO "NO MAN'S LAND". HAVE A PLAYER START AT THE BACK AND WORK IT'S WAY FORWARD TOWARDS THE NET. A PARENT/COACH/PARTNER IS GOING TO FEED THE BALLS EASY AND A PLAYER IS GOING TO HIT IT IN A ZIGZAG PATTERN. STARTING WITH A FOREHAND - THEN BACKHAND - THEN FOREHAND AGAIN AND SO FORTH. REPEAT 15 TIMES ALL THE WAY THROUGH.

FOOTWORK.
DO AT LEAST ONE (1) EXERCISE FROM PAGE 45 - 46, WRITE IT DOWN.

EXERCISE	REPS/MINS/SECS	EXERCISE	REPS/MINS/SECS
. . . .		. . . .	
. . . .		. . . .	

GAME. DODGEBALL.
A COACH/PARENT THROWS BALLS AT A PLAYER AND A PLAYER SHOULD DODGE IT. TIP. DON'T THROW THE BALL HARD AS IT CAN HURT. THE GOAL IS TO MAKE A PLAYER CHANGE DIRECTIONS AS HE/SHE RUNS AROUND AND HAVE FUN.

COOL DOWN.
SLOWLY JOG ONE LAP AROUND THE COURT. . . . .

STRETCH.
TO FINISH OFF THE PRACTICE WE NEED TO STRETCH. THIS WILL HELP TO KEEP MUSCLES FROM GETTING TOO SORE. . . . .

PRACTICE SUMMARY

WHAT I NEED TO WORK ON? . . . .
. . . .
. . . .
. . . .
. . . .
. . . .
. . . .
. . . .
. . . .

COACH'S NOTES: . . . .
. . . .
. . . .
. . . .
. . . .
. . . .
. . . .
. . . .
. . . .

WHAT DID I DO GOOD TODAY? . . . .
. . . .
. . . .
. . . .
. . . .
. . . .
. . . .
. . . .

MY NOTES: . . . .
. . . .
. . . .
. . . .
. . . .
. . . .
. . . .
. . . .
. . . .

IMPORTANT POINTS TO REMEMBER:
- KEEP KNEES BENT.
- KEEP HEELS OFF THE COURT.
- WHEN MAKING A SWING AND HITTING A BALL ELBOWS SHOULD NOT TOUCH A PLAYER'S STOMACH AREA.
- KEEP ELBOWS SLIGHTLY BENT (ALMOST STRAIGHT).
- DON'T FORGET TO FOLLOW THROUGH AFTER CONTACT WITH THE BALL.

RATE LESSON:

☆ ☆ ☆ ☆ ☆

**GREAT JOB TODAY!
KEEP IT UP!**

LESSON 8

ITEMS NEEDED:
- [ ] RACKET
- [ ] BALLS
- [ ] CONES
- [ ] SPOT MARKERS
- [ ] TENNIS SHOES

OPTIONAL:
- [ ] JUMP ROPE

DATE: __ / __ / __

☹ 😐 😀 😊 😤

WARM UP.

- JOG 3-5 LAPS AROUND THE COURT.

DO AT LEAST EIGHT (8) WARM UP EXERCISES FROM PAGE 35 - 36, WRITE IT DOWN.

EXERCISE	REPS/MINS/SECS	EXERCISE	REPS/MINS/SECS
....	....	....	....
....	....	....	....
....	....	....	....
....	....	....	....
....	....	....	....

STRETCH.

DO AT LEAST THREE (3) STRETCHING EXERCISES FROM PAGE 37, WRITE IT DOWN.

EXERCISE	REPS/MINS/SECS	EXERCISE	REPS/MINS/SECS
....	....	....	....
....	....	....	....
....	....	....	....

HAND - EYE COORDINATION.

THE GAME OF TENNIS REQUIRES GREAT HAND-EYE COORDINATION. TENNIS PLAYERS WORK ON IT ALL THROUGHOUT THEIR TENNIS CAREERS. INDEED, IT'S IMPORTANT RIGHT NOW, AS YOU BEGIN YOUR TENNIS JOURNEY.

DO AT LEAST TWO (2) EXERCISES FROM THE LIST ON PAGE 26 - 27, RECORD IT.

EXERCISE	REPS/MINS/SECS	EXERCISE	REPS/MINS/SECS
....	....	....	....
....	....	....	....

REACTION TIME.

ANOTHER IMPORTANT SKILL TO HAVE IS A FAST REACTION TIME. DO AT LEAST TWO (2) EXERCISES FROM THE LIST ON PAGE 24 -25, WRITE IT DOWN.

EXERCISE	REPS/MINS/SECS	EXERCISE	REPS/MINS/SECS
....	....	....	....
....	....	....	....
....	....	....	....

REVIEW. VOLLEY.

START BY ALTERNATING FOREHAND AND BACKHAND BLOCK VOLLEYS. REMEMBER TO MOVE YOUR FEET AND GET TO THE BALL. A BALL IS NOT GOING TO COME TO YOU. REPEAT 50 TIMES. ....

LESSON 8

REVIEW. GROUND STROKES.
CONTINUE WITH ALTERNATING FOREHAND AND BACKHAND GROUND STROKES FROM A SERVICE LINE. THIS TIME A COACH/PARENT SHOULD START FEEDING EASY BALLS FROM ACROSS THE NET. REPEAT 50 TIMES. . . . .

RUN ONE LAP AROUND THE COURT AS FAST AS POSSIBLE ON TIME. A PARENT/COACH START A TIMER. RECORD YOUR RESULTS: . . . .

DRILL. HOP SCOTCH.
WE ARE GOING TO COMBINE GROUND STROKES WITH VOLLEYS. SET UP FIVE (5) SPOT MARKERS BEHIND THE SERVICE LINE, IN A PATTERN ONE FOOT - TWO FEET - ONE FOOT. ONE SPOT MARKER A FEW FEET FROM THE NET, AS A VISUAL CUE AND A REMINDER FOR A PLAYER.
A PLAYER SHOULD START BY HOPPING ON SPOT MARKERS, LAND WITH BOTH FEET IN A SPLIT STEP, THEN HIT A FOREHAND AND A BACKHAND GROUND STROKES FROM THE SERVICE LINE. DO A SPLIT STEP AGAIN IN THE CENTER AND RUN TO THE NET TO HIT TWO VOLLEYS. REPEAT 15 TIMES. . . . .
YOU ARE DOING AMAZING!

FOOTWORK.
DO AT LEAST ONE (1) EXERCISE FROM PAGE 45 - 46, WRITE IT DOWN.

EXERCISE	REPS/MINS/SECS	EXERCISE	REPS/MINS/SECS
. . . .	. . . .	. . . .	. . . .
. . . .	. . . .	. . . .	. . . .

SERVICE.
I KNOW YOU HAVE BEEN WAITING FOR IT. SERVICE IS THE MOST IMPORTANT STROKE IN TENNIS BECAUSE IT STARTS A GAME. IT IS ALSO THE MOST DIFFICULT ONE. PROFESSIONAL TENNIS PLAYERS SPEND UP TO AN HOUR DURING EACH PRACTICE JUST TO PERFECT A BALL TOSS. I SUGGEST YOU KEEP A TENNIS BALL IN YOUR POCKET AT ALL TIMES WHEN OFF THE COURT. TOSS IT EVERY TIME YOU GET A FREE MINUTE.

THROW BALLS.
FIRST THINGS FIRST, WE ARE GOING TO LEARN TO TOSS A BALL.

FROM THE SERVICE LINE, THROW 20-30 BALLS WITH YOUR DOMINANT ARM DIAGONALLY ACROSS THE NET. . . . .
*RIGHT-HAND DOMINANT PLAYERS, PUT YOUR LEFT FOOT CLOSE TO THE SERVICE LINE, BUT NOT ON IT. IT SHOULD POINT AT THE RIGHT NET POST.
*LEFT-HAND DOMINANT PLAYERS, PUT YOUR RIGHT FOOT CLOSE TO THE SERVICE LINE, BUT NOT ON IT. IT SHOULD POINT AT THE LEFT NET POST.

FROM THIS POSITION, TOSS A BALL UP WITH YOUR NON-DOMINANT HAND ABOVE YOUR HEAD, SLIGHTLY IN FRONT OF YOU AND HIT IT WITH THE OTHER HAND. AT THE POINT OF CONTACT WITH THE BALL YOUR ARM SHOULD BE STRAIGHT. REPEAT 25 - 30 TIMES. . . . .
FOR THE TECHNIQUE ON HOW TO TOSS THE BALL PROPERLY, SEE PAGE 49.

LESSON 8

COOL DOWN.
SLOWLY JOG ONE LAP AROUND THE COURT. . . . .

STRETCH.
TO FINISH OFF THE PRACTICE WE NEED TO STRETCH. THIS WILL HELP TO KEEP
MUSCLES FROM GETTING TOO SORE. . . . .

PRACTICE SUMMARY
WHAT I NEED TO WORK ON? . . . .
. . . .
. . . .
. . . .
. . . .
. . . .

COACH'S NOTES: . . . .
. . . .
. . . .
. . . .
. . . .
. . . .
. . . .

WHAT DID I DO GOOD TODAY? . . . .
. . . .
. . . .
. . . .
. . . .
. . . .
. . . .

MY NOTES: . . . .
. . . .
. . . .
. . . .
. . . .
. . . .
. . . .

IMPORTANT POINTS TO REMEMBER:
- KEEP KNEES BENT.
- KEEP HEELS OFF THE COURT.
- WHEN MAKING A SWING AND HITTING A BALL ELBOWS
  SHOULD NOT TOUCH A PLAYER'S STOMACH AREA.
- KEEP ELBOWS SLIGHTLY BENT (ALMOST STRAIGHT).
- DON'T FORGET TO FOLLOW THROUGH AFTER CONTACT
  WITH THE BALL.

RATE LESSON:

☆ ☆ ☆ ☆ ☆

GREAT JOB TODAY!
KEEP IT UP!

ITEMS NEEDED:
- [ ] RACKET   SPOT MARKERS
- [ ] BALLS   TENNIS SHOES
- [ ] CONES

OPTIONAL:
- [ ] JUMP ROPE

DATE: __ / __ / __

WARM UP.
- JOG 3-5 LAPS AROUND THE COURT.

DO AT LEAST EIGHT (8) WARM UP EXERCISES FROM PAGE 35 - 36, WRITE IT DOWN.

EXERCISE	REPS/MINS/SECS	EXERCISE	REPS/MINS/SECS
....	....	....	....
....	....	....	....
....	....	....	....
....	....	....	....
....	....	....	....

STRETCH.
DO AT LEAST THREE (3) STRETCHING EXERCISES FROM PAGE 37, WRITE IT DOWN.

EXERCISE	REPS/MINS/SECS	EXERCISE	REPS/MINS/SECS
....	....	....	....
....	....	....	....
....	....	....	....

HAND - EYE COORDINATION.
THE GAME OF TENNIS REQUIRES GREAT HAND-EYE COORDINATION. TENNIS PLAYERS WORK ON IT ALL THROUGHOUT THEIR TENNIS CAREERS. INDEED, IT'S IMPORTANT RIGHT NOW, AS YOU BEGIN YOUR TENNIS JOURNEY.

DO AT LEAST TWO (2) EXERCISES FROM THE LIST ON PAGE 26 - 27, RECORD IT.

EXERCISE	REPS/MINS/SECS	EXERCISE	REPS/MINS/SECS
....	....	....	....
....	....	....	....

REACTION TIME.
ANOTHER IMPORTANT SKILL TO HAVE IS A FAST REACTION TIME. DO AT LEAST TWO (2) EXERCISES FROM THE LIST ON PAGE 24 -25, WRITE IT DOWN.

EXERCISE	REPS/MINS/SECS	EXERCISE	REPS/MINS/SECS
....	....	....	....
....	....	....	....
....	....	....	....

BALL CONTROL. DRILL 1.

A PLAYER AND A COACH START ON THE OPPOSITE SIDES OF THE NET, BOTH ARE 5-6 FEET AWAY FROM IT. HIT VERY EASY AND GENTLE BALLS TO EACH OTHER. THE GOAL IS TO HIT AT LEAST 10 BALLS UNINTERRUPTED.
TIP. RELAX YOUR HAND AND DON'T TRY TO HIT HARD.

THIS EXERCISE WILL TEACH YOU TO CONTROL HOW HARD YOU CAN HIT THE BALLS. SOMETIMES IT'S A GOOD IDEA TO CATCH AN OPPONENT BY SURPRISE WITH A SHORT BALL. IN FACT, HITTING A SHORT AND GENTLE BALL CAN BE MORE DIFFICULT THAN USING ALL YOUR STRENGTH.

BALL CONTROL. DRILL 2.

A COACH FEEDS THE BALLS EASILY. A PLAYER IS AT THE SERVICE LINE.
SET UP 3-5 CONES IN BOTH CORNERS (DEUCE AND ADVANTAGE SIDES) OF THE SERVICE LINE ON THE OPPOSITE SIDE FROM A PLAYER. HIT 50 FOREHAND GROUND STROKES DIAGONALLY. SWITCH TO BACKHAND. HIT 50 BACKHANDS DIAGONALLY. A PLAYER SHOULD AIM AT HITTING THE CONES.
HOW MANY CONES DID YOU HIT? . . . .
. . . .
FANTASTIC JOB!

SPIDER RUN.

SEE DESCRIPTION OF THIS EXERCISE ON PAGE 48.
RECORD YOUR RESULTS. . . . .
. . . .

BALL CONTROL. DRILL 3.

A COACH FEEDS THE BALLS EASILY FROM ACROSS THE NET IN A FOLLOWING PATTERN.
FOREHAND - "NO MAN'S LAND". . . . .
BACKHAND - SERVICE LINE. . . . .
VOLLEY - FOREHAND . . . .
A PLAYER SHOULD RUN AND HIT ALL THREE BALLS INTO THE OPPOSITE SIDE OF THE COURT.

TIP.
YOU CAN SET UP SPOT MARKERS AS VISUAL CUES AND REMINDERS FOR A PLAYER AS TO WHERE TO RUN AND HIT A BALL NEXT.
REPEAT THIS DRILL AT LEAST 10 TIMES. . . . .

SERVICE.
I HOPE YOU HAVE BEEN PRACTICING TOSSING A BALL UP TO THE EYE LEVEL AND CATCHING IT. TODAY WE ARE GOING TO TOSS A BALL EVEN HIGHER. READ ABOUT HOW TO TOSS A BALL ON PAGE 49.

SET UP A SPOT MARKER IN "NO MAN'S LAND", BETWEEN A SERVICE LINE AND A BASELINE SLIGHTLY OFF THE CENTER. GET IN A POSITION, PUT LEFT FOOT (RIGHT FOOT FOR LEFTIES) TO IT, BUT DON'T STEP ON IT. EXTEND YOUR LEFT ARM (RIGHT ARM FOR LEFTIES) IN FRONT OF YOU AND TOSS A BALL UP ABOVE YOUR HEAD AND CATCH IT. REPEAT 20 TIMES.

HOLD A RACKET WITH YOUR DOMINANT HAND, WITH A CONTINENTAL GRIP. TOSS A BALL UP AND AS IT TRAVELS TO ITS HIGHEST POINT, BEND YOUR DOMINANT ARM BEHIND YOUR BACK, EXTEND YOUR ELBOW UP AND HIT THE BALL WHILE IT'S AT THE HIGHEST POINT. A PLAYER SHOULD THRIVE TO HIT A BALL WITH AN ALMOST STRAIGHT ARM. REPEAT 25 - 30 TIMES. . . . .

GREAT JOB!
KEEP PRACTICING A BALL TOSS AND CATCH AT HOME IN BETWEEN THE CLASSES.

FOOTWORK.
DO AT LEAST ONE (1) EXERCISE FROM PAGE 45 - 46, WRITE IT DOWN.

EXERCISE	REPS/MINS/SECS	EXERCISE	REPS/MINS/SECS
. . . .		. . . .	
. . . .		. . . .	

GAME. RALLY.
START ON THE OPPOSITE SIDES OF THE NET, BOTH ARE AT THE SERVICE LINE. A COACH AND A PLAYER SHOULD HIT THE BALLS TO EACH OTHER. THIS IS YOUR FIRST RALLY. TRY TO KEEP A BALL IN THE GAME FOR AS LONG AS POSSIBLE. UTILIZE BOTH FOREHAND AND BACKHAND STROKES. AIM FOR 6 UNINTERRUPTED SHOTS. GREAT JOB!

COOL DOWN.
SLOWLY JOG ONE LAP AROUND THE COURT. . . . .

STRETCH.
TO FINISH OFF THE PRACTICE WE NEED TO STRETCH. THIS WILL HELP TO KEEP MUSCLES FROM GETTING TOO SORE. . . . .

LESSON 9

PRACTICE SUMMARY

WHAT I NEED TO WORK ON? ....
....
....
....
....
....
....
....
....

COACH'S NOTES: ....
....
....
....
....
....
....
....
....

WHAT DID I DO GOOD TODAY? ....
....
....
....
....
....
....
....
....

MY NOTES: ....
....
....
....
....
....
....
....

IMPORTANT POINTS TO REMEMBER:

- KEEP KNEES BENT.
- KEEP HEELS OFF THE COURT.
- WHEN MAKING A SWING AND HITTING A BALL ELBOWS SHOULD NOT TOUCH A PLAYER'S STOMACH AREA.
- KEEP ELBOWS SLIGHTLY BENT (ALMOST STRAIGHT).
- DON'T FORGET TO FOLLOW THROUGH AFTER CONTACT WITH THE BALL.

RATE LESSON:

☆☆☆☆☆

GREAT JOB TODAY! KEEP IT UP!

LESSON 10

ITEMS NEEDED:

☐ RACKET   SPOT MARKERS
☐ BALLS   TENNIS SHOES
☐ CONES

OPTIONAL:

☐ JUMP ROPE

DATE: __ / __ / __

☹ 🙁 😐 🙂 😁

WARM UP.

- JOG 3-5 LAPS AROUND THE COURT.

DO AT LEAST EIGHT (8) WARM UP EXERCISES FROM PAGE 35 - 36, WRITE IT DOWN.

EXERCISE	REPS/MINS/SECS	EXERCISE	REPS/MINS/SECS
....		....	
....		....	
....		....	
....		....	
....		....	

STRETCH.

DO AT LEAST THREE (3) STRETCHING EXERCISES FROM PAGE 37, WRITE IT DOWN.

EXERCISE	REPS/MINS/SECS	EXERCISE	REPS/MINS/SECS
....		....	
....		....	
....		....	

HAND - EYE COORDINATION.

THE GAME OF TENNIS REQUIRES GREAT HAND-EYE COORDINATION. TENNIS PLAYERS WORK ON IT ALL THROUGHOUT THEIR TENNIS CAREERS. INDEED, IT'S IMPORTANT RIGHT NOW, AS YOU BEGIN YOUR TENNIS JOURNEY.

DO AT LEAST TWO (2) EXERCISES FROM THE LIST ON PAGE 26 - 27, RECORD IT.

EXERCISE	REPS/MINS/SECS	EXERCISE	REPS/MINS/SECS
....		....	
....		....	

DRILL 1. CONTROL THE BALL.

SET UP A CONE IN THE CENTER OF THE "NO MAN'S LAND". SET UP CONES OR BALL CANS ON THE OTHER SIDE OF THE COURT. A COACH/PARENT FEEDS BALLS FROM ACROSS THE NET. A PLAYER SHOULD START WITH A BACKHAND STROKES AND AIM AT THE CONES CROSS COURT. THEN SHUFFLE AROUND THE CONE, DO A SPLIT STEP AND HIT ANOTHER BACKHAND. REPEAT 30 TIMES. ....
....
SWITCH. FROM THE SAME POSITION, HIT 30 FOREHAND STROKES AND AIM AT THE CONES CROSS COURT. ....
....
....
AWESOME!

RUN AROUND THE COURT AND WHEN A COACH/PARENT CLAPS HANDS AND SAYS BURPEE, A PLAYER STOPS, DOES A BURPEE AND CONTINUES TO RUN. A PLAYER SHOULD DO AT LEAST SIX(6) BURPEES AROUND ONE COURT. . . . . ☐
. . . .

DRILL 2.
CONTINUE FROM A "NO MAN'S LAND " HIT BALLS IN A FOLLOWING PATTERN:
FOREHAND . . . .
THEN BACKHAND. . . . .
THEN SHORT BALL FROM THE SERVICE LINE EITHER FOREHAND OR BACKHAND
(A COACH SHOULD ALTERNATE) . . . .
TWO BLOCK VOLLEYS, FOREHAND AND BACKHAND. REPEAT THIS DRILL 10 TIMES. .
. . . .

FOOTWORK.
A COACH STARTS THE TIMER. A PLAYER RUNS TO AND TOUCHES THE SERVICE LINE, COMES BACK TO THE BASELINE. THEN RUN TO THE NET AND BACK. TAKE A 30 SECOND BREAK AND REPEAT. RECORD THE BEST OF TWO RESULTS. . . . .
. . . .

SERVICE.
- 10 MINUTES TO TOSS THE BALLS UP AND CATCH IT WITH NON-DOMINANT HAND. . . . .
- 10 MINUTES TO TOSS BALLS AND MAKE A BACKSWING. BUT DON'T HIT THE BALLS JUST YET. . . . .
- COMBINE THE BALL TOSS, A BACKSWING AND HIT A SERVICE. SPEND AT LEAST ANOTHER 10-20 MINUTES. . . . .
. . . .

GAME. RALLY.
- FROM THE SERVICE LINE START BY RALLYING DIAGONALLY ACROSS THE NET.
- A) FOREHAND - TO - FOREHAND . . . .
- B) BACKHAND - TO - BACKHAND. . . . .
- STRIVE FOR 10-15 UNINTERRUPTED STROKES ON EACH SIDE. . . . .
. . . .

COOL DOWN.
SLOWLY JOG ONE LAP AROUND THE COURT. . . . .

STRETCH.
TO FINISH OFF THE PRACTICE WE NEED TO STRETCH. THIS WILL HELP TO KEEP MUSCLES FROM GETTING TOO SORE. . . . .

LESSON 10

PRACTICE SUMMARY

WHAT I NEED TO WORK ON? . . . .
. . . .
. . . .
. . . .
. . . .
. . . .
. . . .
. . . .

COACH'S NOTES: . . . .
. . . .
. . . .
. . . .
. . . .
. . . .
. . . .

WHAT DID I DO GOOD TODAY? . . . .
. . . .
. . . .
. . . .
. . . .
. . . .

MY NOTES: . . . .
. . . .
. . . .
. . . .
. . . .
. . . .
. . . .
. . . .

IMPORTANT POINTS TO REMEMBER:

- KEEP KNEES BENT.
- KEEP HEELS OFF THE COURT.
- WHEN MAKING A SWING AND HITTING A BALL ELBOWS SHOULD NOT TOUCH A PLAYER'S STOMACH AREA.
- KEEP ELBOWS SLIGHTLY BENT (ALMOST STRAIGHT).
- DON'T FORGET TO FOLLOW THROUGH AFTER CONTACT WITH THE BALL.

RATE LESSON:

GREAT JOB TODAY! KEEP IT UP!

LESSON 11

ITEMS NEEDED:

☐ RACKET ☐ SPOT MARKERS
☐ BALLS ☐ TENNIS SHOES
☐ CONES

OPTIONAL:

☐ JUMP ROPE

DATE: __ / __ / __

☹ ☺ 😐 😊 🤩

WARM UP.

- JOG 3-5 LAPS AROUND THE COURT.

DO AT LEAST EIGHT (8) WARM UP EXERCISES FROM PAGE 35 - 36, WRITE IT DOWN.

EXERCISE	REPS/MINS/SECS	EXERCISE	REPS/MINS/SECS
....		....	
....		....	
....		....	
....		....	
....		....	

STRETCH.

DO AT LEAST THREE (3) STRETCHING EXERCISES FROM PAGE 37, WRITE IT DOWN.

EXERCISE	REPS/MINS/SECS	EXERCISE	REPS/MINS/SECS
....		....	
....		....	
....		....	

HAND - EYE COORDINATION.

THE GAME OF TENNIS REQUIRES GREAT HAND-EYE COORDINATION. TENNIS PLAYERS WORK ON IT ALL THROUGHOUT THEIR TENNIS CAREERS. INDEED, IT'S IMPORTANT RIGHT NOW, AS YOU BEGIN YOUR TENNIS JOURNEY.

DO AT LEAST TWO (2) EXERCISES FROM THE LIST ON PAGE 26 - 27, RECORD IT.

EXERCISE	REPS/MINS/SECS	EXERCISE	REPS/MINS/SECS
....		....	
....		....	

REACTION TIME.

ANOTHER IMPORTANT SKILL TO HAVE IS A FAST REACTION TIME. DO AT LEAST TWO (2) EXERCISES FROM THE LIST ON PAGE 24 -25, WRITE IT DOWN.

EXERCISE	REPS/MINS/SECS	EXERCISE	REPS/MINS/SECS
....		....	
....		....	
....		....	

SERVICE.

- FROM THE BASELINE, SPEND 10 MINUTES TOSSING THE BALLS UP AND CATCHING IT WITH NON-DOMINANT HAND.

SERVICE.

- ADD A BACKSWING TO IT. SPEND 10 MINUTES TO TOSS THE BALL AND BACKSWING TO THE TROPHY POSE. TO REFRESH YOUR KNOWLEDGE ABOUT THE BACKSWING AND A TROPHY POSE SEE PAGE 43 - 44.
- SPEND 20 MINUTES TO WORK ON A FULL SERVICE. TOSS A BALL, BACKSWING AND HIT A BALL.

RUN ONE LAP AROUND THE COURT AS FAST AS POSSIBLE ON TIME. A PARENT/COACH START A TIMER. RECORD YOUR RESULTS: . . . .

FOOTWORK.

DO AT LEAST ONE (1) EXERCISE FROM PAGE 45 - 46, WRITE IT DOWN.

EXERCISE	REPS/MINS/SECS	EXERCISE	REPS/MINS/SECS
. . . .		. . . .	
. . . .		. . . .	

GAME. RALLY.

FROM THE SERVICE LINE START BY RALLYING DIAGONALLY ACROSS THE NET.

A) FOREHAND - TO - FOREHAND . . . .

B) BACKHAND - TO - BACKHAND . . . .

STRIVE FOR 10-15 UNINTERRUPTED STROKES ON EACH SIDE. . . . .

. . . .

GAME. POPCORN.

PUT A FEW BALLS AS YOU CAN FIT ON A TENNIS RACKET WITHOUT IT FALLING OFF THE RACKET. A COACH/PARENT THROWS THE BALLS UP FROM A RACKET ALL AT ONCE AND A PLAYER SHOULD RUN AND CATCH AS MANY AS HE CAN WITH A CONE BEFORE THE BALLS BOUNCE . . . .

COOL DOWN.

SLOWLY JOG ONE LAP AROUND THE COURT. . . . .

STRETCH.

TO FINISH OFF THE PRACTICE WE NEED TO STRETCH. THIS WILL HELP TO KEEP MUSCLES FROM GETTING TOO SORE. . . . .

LESSON 11

PRACTICE SUMMARY

WHAT I NEED TO WORK ON? . . . .
. . . .
. . . .
. . . .
. . . .
. . . .
. . . .
. . . .
. . . .

COACH'S NOTES: . . . .
. . . .
. . . .
. . . .
. . . .
. . . .
. . . .
. . . .
. . . .

WHAT DID I DO GOOD TODAY? . . . .
. . . .
. . . .
. . . .
. . . .
. . . .
. . . .
. . . .

MY NOTES: . . . .
. . . .
. . . .
. . . .
. . . .
. . . .
. . . .
. . . .

IMPORTANT POINTS TO REMEMBER:

- KEEP KNEES BENT.
- KEEP HEELS OFF THE COURT.
- WHEN MAKING A SWING AND HITTING A BALL ELBOWS SHOULD NOT TOUCH A PLAYER'S STOMACH AREA.
- KEEP ELBOWS SLIGHTLY BENT (ALMOST STRAIGHT).
- DON'T FORGET TO FOLLOW THROUGH AFTER CONTACT WITH THE BALL.

RATE LESSON:

☆ ☆ ☆ ☆ ☆

**GREAT JOB TODAY!
KEEP IT UP!**

LESSON 12

ITEMS NEEDED:

☐ RACKET ☐ SPOT MARKERS
☐ BALLS ☐ TENNIS SHOES
☐ CONES

OPTIONAL:

☐ JUMP ROPE

DATE: __ / __ / __

😟 😐 😄 😌 😴

WARM UP.

- JOG 3-5 LAPS AROUND THE COURT.

DO AT LEAST EIGHT (8) WARM UP EXERCISES FROM PAGE 35 - 36, WRITE IT DOWN.

EXERCISE	REPS/MINS/SECS	EXERCISE	REPS/MINS/SECS
....	....	....	....
....	....	....	....
....	....	....	....
....	....	....	....
....	....	....	....

STRETCH.

DO AT LEAST THREE (3) STRETCHING EXERCISES FROM PAGE 37, WRITE IT DOWN.

EXERCISE	REPS/MINS/SECS	EXERCISE	REPS/MINS/SECS
....	....	....	....
....	....	....	....
....	....	....	....

HAND - EYE COORDINATION.

THE GAME OF TENNIS REQUIRES GREAT HAND-EYE COORDINATION. TENNIS PLAYERS WORK ON IT ALL THROUGHOUT THEIR TENNIS CAREERS. INDEED, IT'S IMPORTANT RIGHT NOW, AS YOU BEGIN YOUR TENNIS JOURNEY.

DO AT LEAST TWO (2) EXERCISES FROM THE LIST ON PAGE 26 - 27, RECORD IT.

EXERCISE	REPS/MINS/SECS	EXERCISE	REPS/MINS/SECS
....	....	....	....
....	....	....	....

VOLLEYS.

ALTERNATE FOREHAND AND BACKHAND BLOCK VOLLEYS. REPEAT 30 - 50 TIMES:
....

GROUNDSTROKES.

ALTERNATE BETWEEN FOREHAND AND BACKHAND GROUND STROKES FROM THE SERVICE LINE. REPEAT 30 - 50 TIMES: ....
....

RUN ONE LAP AROUND THE COURT AS FAST AS POSSIBLE ON TIME. A PARENT/COACH START A TIMER. RECORD YOUR RESULTS: ....
....

LESSON 12

BASELINE.
STARTING IN THE CENTER OF THE BASELINE:
HIT CROSS - COURT FOREHAND STROKES. REPEAT 30 TIMES: . . . .
. . . .
HIT CROSS - COURT BACKHAND STROKES. REPEAT 30 TIMES: . . . .

DRILL 1.
A COACH FEEDS EASY BALLS FROM ACROSS THE NET IN A FOLLOWING PATTERN:
BASELINE - FOREHAND . . . .
BASELINE - BACKHAND . . . .
HALF-COURT - FOREHAND . . . .
TWO ALTERNATING VOLLEYS. . . . .
REPEAT THE DRILL 15 TIMES.

DRILL 2.
A COACH/PARENT FEEDS THE BALLS EASY FROM ACROSS THE NET IN A FOLLOWING
PATTERN.
BASELINE BACKHAND . . . .
HALF-COURT FOREHAND . . . .
BACKHAND VOLLEY. . . . .
REPEAT THE DRILL 15 TIMES.

TIP.
YOU CAN PLACE SPOT MARKERS TO GIVE A PLAYER VISUAL CUES WHERE TO MOVE
NEXT.

FOOTWORK
SHUFFLE SIDEWAYS FROM THE CENTER LINE TO THE SINGLES LINE FOR 30 SECONDS
AS FAST AS POSSIBLE. COUNT HOW MANY TIMES YOU TAP EACH LINE. RECORD
YOUR RESULTS. . . . .
. . . .

SERVICE.
PRACTICE THE SERVICE FOR AT LEAST 20 MINUTES. . . . .
. . . .

GAME. RALLY.
FROM THE SERVICE LINE START BY RALLYING DIAGONALLY ACROSS THE NET.
A) FOREHAND - TO - FOREHAND . . . .
B) BACKHAND - TO - BACKHAND . . . .
STRIVE FOR 10-15 UNINTERRUPTED STROKES ON EACH SIDE . . . .
. . . .

LESSON 12

COOL DOWN.
SLOWLY JOG ONE LAP AROUND THE COURT.....................................

STRETCH.
TO FINISH OFF THE PRACTICE WE NEED TO STRETCH. THIS WILL HELP TO KEEP
MUSCLES FROM GETTING TOO SORE...

PRACTICE SUMMARY
WHAT I NEED TO WORK ON?..
....
....
....
....
....

COACH'S NOTES:..
....
....
....
....
....
....

WHAT DID I DO GOOD TODAY?...
....
....
....
....
....

MY NOTES:...
....
....
....
....
....
....

IMPORTANT POINTS TO REMEMBER:
- KEEP KNEES BENT.
- KEEP HEELS OFF THE COURT.
- WHEN MAKING A SWING AND HITTING A BALL ELBOWS
  SHOULD NOT TOUCH A PLAYER'S STOMACH AREA.
- KEEP ELBOWS SLIGHTLY BENT (ALMOST STRAIGHT).
- DON'T FORGET TO FOLLOW THROUGH AFTER CONTACT
  WITH THE BALL.

RATE LESSON:
☆☆☆☆☆

**GREAT JOB TODAY!
KEEP IT UP!**

ITEMS NEEDED:

- [ ] RACKET
- [ ] BALLS
- [ ] CONES
- [ ] SPOT MARKERS
- [ ] TENNIS SHOES

OPTIONAL:

- [ ] JUMP ROPE

DATE: _ / _ / _

😞 😐 😃 😊 😎

WARM UP.

- JOG 3-5 LAPS AROUND THE COURT.

DO AT LEAST EIGHT (8) WARM UP EXERCISES FROM PAGE 35 - 36, WRITE IT DOWN.

EXERCISE	REPS/MINS/SECS	EXERCISE	REPS/MINS/SECS
....	....	....	....
....	....	....	....
....	....	....	....
....	....	....	....
....	....	....	....

STRETCH.

DO AT LEAST THREE (3) STRETCHING EXERCISES FROM PAGE 37, WRITE IT DOWN.

EXERCISE	REPS/MINS/SECS	EXERCISE	REPS/MINS/SECS
....	....	....	....
....	....	....	....
....	....	....	....

HAND - EYE COORDINATION.

THE GAME OF TENNIS REQUIRES GREAT HAND-EYE COORDINATION. TENNIS PLAYERS WORK ON IT ALL THROUGHOUT THEIR TENNIS CAREERS. INDEED, IT'S IMPORTANT RIGHT NOW, AS YOU BEGIN YOUR TENNIS JOURNEY.

DO AT LEAST TWO (2) EXERCISES FROM THE LIST ON PAGE 26 - 27, RECORD IT.

EXERCISE	REPS/MINS/SECS	EXERCISE	REPS/MINS/SECS
....	....	....	....
....	....	....	....

TODAY WE ARE GOING TO PLAY POINTS! YAY!
FIRST, WE NEED TO WARM UP ALL THE STROKES THAT WE ARE GOING TO USE DURING A GAME, VOLLEYS, FOREHAND AND BACKHAND GROUND STROKES AND A SERVICE.

START AT THE NET AND HIT 30 - 50 VOLLEYS. NEXT UP, FROM THE SERVICE LINE, HIT FOREHAND AND BACKHAND STROKES. MOVE TO THE BASELINE AS YOU CONTINUE TO WARM UP.

RUN AROUND THE COURT AND WHEN A COACH/PARENT CLAPS HANDS AND SAYS BURPEE, A PLAYER STOPS, DOES A BURPEE AND CONTINUES TO RUN. A PLAYER SHOULD DO AT LEAST SIX(6) BURPEES AROUND ONE COURT............... [ ]
....

SERVICE.
HIT A FEW WARM UP SERVES. ONCE YOU GET COMFORTABLE AND ARE READY TO
PLAY, START SERVING. . . . .
. . . .
. . . .

MATCH. ROUND 1.
A PLAYER SERVES A BALL TO THE COACH/PARENT AND IF THE BALL MAKES IT INTO
A CORRECT SERVICE BOX, AN OPPONENT RETURNS IT. CONTINUE TO RALLY UNTIL
ONE OF THE PLAYERS WINS A POINT. START FROM THE DEUCE SIDE. CONTINUE TO
TEN (10) POINTS WITH A DIFFERENCE IN 2. FOR EXAMPLE, 10-8.
AWESOME JOB!

FOOTWORK.
MOVING FAST ON A COURT IS A MUST FOR ANY TENNIS PLAYER. IN ORDER TO BE
READY TO ACCELERATE AT ANY MOMENT DURING A MATCH, PLAYERS NEED TO ADD
SPRINTS TO THEIR TRAINING ROUTINES.

SPRINT DIAGONALLY CROSS COURT FROM THE NET TO THE BASELINE. RECORD
YOUR RESULTS: . . . .
. . . .
. . . .

MATCH. ROUND 2.
A COACH/PARENT SERVES AND A PLAYER RETURNS IF THE BALL MAKES IT INTO A
CORRECT SERVICE BOX. PLAY TO TEN (10) POINTS.
FANTASTIC!

WHO WON?
RECORD YOUR RESULTS.
DID YOU DO EVERYTHING THAT YOU KNOW SO FAR? WHAT NEEDS IMPROVEMENT?
. . . .
. . . .
. . . .
. . . .
. . . .

COOL DOWN.
SLOWLY JOG ONE LAP AROUND THE COURT. . . . .

STRETCH.
TO FINISH OFF THE PRACTICE WE NEED TO STRETCH. THIS WILL HELP TO KEEP
MUSCLES FROM GETTING TOO SORE. . . . .

PRACTICE SUMMARY

WHAT I NEED TO WORK ON? . . . .
. . . .
. . . .
. . . .
. . . .
. . . .
. . . .
. . . .

COACH'S NOTES: . . . .
. . . .
. . . .
. . . .
. . . .
. . . .
. . . .
. . . .

WHAT DID I DO GOOD TODAY? . . . .
. . . .
. . . .
. . . .
. . . .
. . . .
. . . .
. . . .

MY NOTES: . . . .
. . . .
. . . .
. . . .
. . . .
. . . .
. . . .
. . . .

IMPORTANT POINTS TO REMEMBER:

- KEEP KNEES BENT.
- KEEP HEELS OFF THE COURT.
- WHEN MAKING A SWING AND HITTING A BALL ELBOWS SHOULD NOT TOUCH A PLAYER'S STOMACH AREA.
- KEEP ELBOWS SLIGHTLY BENT (ALMOST STRAIGHT).
- DON'T FORGET TO FOLLOW THROUGH AFTER CONTACT WITH THE BALL.

RATE LESSON:

☆☆☆☆☆

**GREAT JOB TODAY!
KEEP IT UP!**

LESSON 14

ITEMS NEEDED:
- [ ] RACKET
- [ ] BALLS
- [ ] CONES
- [ ] SPOT MARKERS
- [ ] TENNIS SHOES

OPTIONAL:
- [ ] JUMP ROPE

DATE: __ / __ / __

☹ 😐 😊 😌 😎

WARM UP.
- JOG 3-5 LAPS AROUND THE COURT.

DO AT LEAST EIGHT (8) WARM UP EXERCISES FROM PAGE 35 - 36, WRITE IT DOWN.

EXERCISE	REPS/MINS/SECS	EXERCISE	REPS/MINS/SECS
....		....	
....		....	
....		....	
....		....	
....		....	

STRETCH.
DO AT LEAST THREE (3) STRETCHING EXERCISES FROM PAGE 37, WRITE IT DOWN.

EXERCISE	REPS/MINS/SECS	EXERCISE	REPS/MINS/SECS
....		....	
....		....	
....		....	

HAND - EYE COORDINATION.
THE GAME OF TENNIS REQUIRES GREAT HAND-EYE COORDINATION. TENNIS PLAYERS WORK ON IT ALL THROUGHOUT THEIR TENNIS CAREERS. INDEED, IT'S IMPORTANT RIGHT NOW, AS YOU BEGIN YOUR TENNIS JOURNEY.

DO AT LEAST TWO (2) EXERCISES FROM THE LIST ON PAGE 26 - 27, RECORD IT.

EXERCISE	REPS/MINS/SECS	EXERCISE	REPS/MINS/SECS
....		....	
....		....	

REACTION TIME.
ANOTHER IMPORTANT SKILL TO HAVE IS A FAST REACTION TIME. DO AT LEAST TWO (2) EXERCISES FROM THE LIST ON PAGE 24 -25, WRITE IT DOWN.

EXERCISE	REPS/MINS/SECS	EXERCISE	REPS/MINS/SECS
....		....	
....		....	
....		....	

DRILL 1. HOPSCOTCH.
- SET UP THREE (3) SPOT MARKERS BEHIND THE BASELINE, IN A HOPSCOTCH PATTERN: ONE FOOT - TWO FEET - ONE FOOT.
- ON THE OPPOSITE SIDE OF THE COURT SET UP THREE TO FIVE CONES IN THE CORNERS OF THE BASELINE ON BOTH ADVANTAGE AND DEUCE SIDES.
- A PLAYER SHOULD START WITH A HOPSCOTCH AND LAND ON A BASELINE WITH A SPLIT STEP. ....

LESSON 14

HIT A FOREHAND AND A BACKHAND STROKES CROSS COURT TWO TIMES EACH. AIM AT THE CONES...
RUN TO THE SERVICE LINE AND HIT A BACKHAND................................
RUN TO THE SERVICE LINE AND HIT A BACKHAND AND FOREHAND GROUND STROKES ....
ADVANCE TO THE NET AND HIT A FOREHAND BLOCK VOLLEY...................
REPEAT 6 TIMES...
REMEMBER. DO A SPLIT STEP IN THE CENTER BETWEEN EACH STROKE.

RUN ONE LAP AROUND THE COURT AS FAST AS POSSIBLE ON TIME. A PARENT/COACH START A TIMER. RECORD YOUR RESULTS: ....

DRILL 2. BUTTERFLY.
STARTING AT A BASELINE, A PLAYER HITS A BALL IN A FOLLOWING PATTERN:
FOREHAND FROM THE BASELINE ....
FOREHAND FROM THE SERVICE LINE ....
BACKHAND FROM THE BASELINE ....
BACKHAND FROM THE SERVICE LINE ....
ADVANCE TO THE NET AND HIT FOREHAND AND BACKHAND BLOCK VOLLEYS.......
....
REPEAT 6 TIMES. ....

FOOTWORK.
DO AT LEAST ONE (1) EXERCISE FROM PAGE 45 - 46, WRITE IT DOWN.

EXERCISE	REPS/MINS/SECS	EXERCISE	REPS/MINS/SECS
....	....	....	....
....	....	....	....

SERVICE.
SERVE AND PLAY. 2 ROUNDS TO 10 POINTS WITH A DIFFERENCE IN 2.

GAME.
A COACH/PARENT AND A PLAYER STAND ABOUT 5 FEET ACROSS FROM EACH OTHER. BOTH SHUFFLE ALONG THE LINE (BASELINE OR SERVICE LINE) AND TOSS THE BALL TO EACH OTHER. THE BALL SHOULD ONLY BOUNCE ONCE BEFORE CATCHING IT. REPEAT TWO TIMES.

COOL DOWN.
SLOWLY JOG ONE LAP AROUND THE COURT....................................

STRETCH.
TO FINISH OFF THE PRACTICE WE NEED TO STRETCH. THIS WILL HELP TO KEEP MUSCLES FROM GETTING TOO SORE...

LESSON 14

PRACTICE SUMMARY

WHAT I NEED TO WORK ON? ....
....
....
....
....
....
....
....
....

COACH'S NOTES: ....
....
....
....
....
....
....
....
....

WHAT DID I DO GOOD TODAY? ....
....
....
....
....
....
....
....

MY NOTES: ....
....
....
....
....
....
....
....

IMPORTANT POINTS TO REMEMBER:

- KEEP KNEES BENT.
- KEEP HEELS OFF THE COURT.
- WHEN MAKING A SWING AND HITTING A BALL ELBOWS SHOULD NOT TOUCH A PLAYER'S STOMACH AREA.
- KEEP ELBOWS SLIGHTLY BENT (ALMOST STRAIGHT).
- DON'T FORGET TO FOLLOW THROUGH AFTER CONTACT WITH THE BALL.

RATE LESSON:

**GREAT JOB TODAY!
KEEP IT UP!**

LESSON 15

ITEMS NEEDED:
- [ ] RACKET
- [ ] BALLS
- [ ] CONES
- [ ] SPOT MARKERS
- [ ] TENNIS SHOES

OPTIONAL:
- [ ] JUMP ROPE

DATE: __ / __ / __

☹ 😐 😀 😊 🤩

WARM UP.
- JOG 3-5 LAPS AROUND THE COURT.

DO AT LEAST EIGHT (8) WARM UP EXERCISES FROM PAGE 35 - 36, WRITE IT DOWN.

EXERCISE	REPS/MINS/SECS	EXERCISE	REPS/MINS/SECS
....		....	
....		....	
....		....	
....		....	
....		....	

STRETCH.
DO AT LEAST THREE (3) STRETCHING EXERCISES FROM PAGE 37, WRITE IT DOWN.

EXERCISE	REPS/MINS/SECS	EXERCISE	REPS/MINS/SECS
....		....	
....		....	
....		....	

HAND - EYE COORDINATION.
THE GAME OF TENNIS REQUIRES GREAT HAND-EYE COORDINATION. TENNIS PLAYERS WORK ON IT ALL THROUGHOUT THEIR TENNIS CAREERS. INDEED, IT'S IMPORTANT RIGHT NOW, AS YOU BEGIN YOUR TENNIS JOURNEY.

DO AT LEAST TWO (2) EXERCISES FROM THE LIST ON PAGE 26 - 27, RECORD IT.

EXERCISE	REPS/MINS/SECS	EXERCISE	REPS/MINS/SECS
....		....	
....		....	

REACTION TIME.
ANOTHER IMPORTANT SKILL TO HAVE IS A FAST REACTION TIME. DO AT LEAST TWO (2) EXERCISES FROM THE LIST ON PAGE 24 -25, WRITE IT DOWN.

EXERCISE	REPS/MINS/SECS	EXERCISE	REPS/MINS/SECS
....		....	
....		....	
....		....	

SERVICE.
SET UP CONES IN THE SERVICE BOXES ON THE OPPOSITE SIDE OF THE NET FROM A PLAYER. IT SHOULD BE IN THE CORNERS AND AROUND THE CENTER SERVICE LINE. THE GOAL IS TO HIT AS MANY AS POSSIBLE WITH A SERVICE. RECORD YOUR RESULTS: ....

LESSON 15

GROUND STROKES.
SET UP CONES ON THE OPPOSITE SIDE OF THE NET FROM A PLAYER. SET IT UP AT
RANDOM BUT IN A WAY THAT A COACH/PARENT DOESN'T TRIP ON IT. RALLY FROM
THE BASELINE. HIT AS MANY CONES AS POSSIBLE. RECORD YOUR RESULTS. . . . .
. . . .
. . . .
. . . .

RUN AROUND THE COURT AND WHEN A COACH/PARENT CLAPS HANDS AND SAYS
BURPEE, A PLAYER STOPS, DOES A BURPEE AND CONTINUES TO RUN. A PLAYER
SHOULD DO AT LEAST SIX(6) BURPEES AROUND ONE COURT. . . . .
. . . .

MATCH UP TO FOUR GAMES.
A PLAYER AND A COACH/PARENT TAKE TURNS SERVING ONE GAME AT A TIME
EACH. PLAY UP TO FOUR (4) GAMES WITH A DIFFERENCE IN TWO (2). . . . .
. . . .
. . . .
. . . .
. . . .
. . . .

FOOTWORK.
DO AT LEAST ONE (1) EXERCISE FROM PAGE 45 - 46, WRITE IT DOWN.

EXERCISE	REPS/MINS/SECS	EXERCISE	REPS/MINS/SECS
. . . .	. . . .	. . . .	. . . .
. . . .	. . . .	. . . .	. . . .

GAME. DODGEBALL.
A COACH/PARENT HITS THE BALLS EASILY BUT FAST FROM ACROSS THE COURT
AND A PLAYER HAS TO AVOID GETTING HIT. . . . .
. . . .
. . . .
. . . .

COOL DOWN.
SLOWLY JOG ONE LAP AROUND THE COURT. . . . .

STRETCH.
TO FINISH OFF THE PRACTICE WE NEED TO STRETCH. THIS WILL HELP TO KEEP
MUSCLES FROM GETTING TOO SORE. . . . .

LESSON 15

PRACTICE SUMMARY
WHAT I NEED TO WORK ON? . . . .
. . . .
. . . .
. . . .
. . . .
. . . .
. . . .
. . . .
. . . .

COACH'S NOTES: . . . .
. . . .
. . . .
. . . .
. . . .
. . . .
. . . .
. . . .

WHAT DID I DO GOOD TODAY? . . . .
. . . .
. . . .
. . . .
. . . .
. . . .
. . . .

MY NOTES: . . . .
. . . .
. . . .
. . . .
. . . .
. . . .
. . . .
. . . .

IMPORTANT POINTS TO REMEMBER:
- KEEP KNEES BENT.
- KEEP HEELS OFF THE COURT.
- WHEN MAKING A SWING AND HITTING A BALL ELBOWS SHOULD NOT TOUCH A PLAYER'S STOMACH AREA.
- KEEP ELBOWS SLIGHTLY BENT (ALMOST STRAIGHT).
- DON'T FORGET TO FOLLOW THROUGH AFTER CONTACT WITH THE BALL.

RATE LESSON:

☆☆☆☆☆

GREAT JOB TODAY! KEEP IT UP!

CONCLUSION

CONGRATULATIONS! YOU JUST FINISHED YOUR 15TH LESSON! IF YOU FOLLOWED THE INSTRUCTIONS AND REPEATED EVERY LESSON UNTIL THE SKILLS ARE MASTERED, THEN YOU'VE LEARNED HOW TO RALLY, SERVE AND HIT A WINNER VOLLEY. ALONG WITH A FOREHAND AND A BACKHAND GROUND STROKES. COMPLETING THIS PROGRAM IN SIX MONTHS IS NOT A FINAL DESTINATION, THIS IS A BEGINNING. THERE IS SO MUCH TO LEARN AHEAD.

KEEP THIS WORKBOOK HANDY AS THERE'S A LOT OF INFORMATION, DRILLS AND EXERCISES THAT YOU CAN LOOK BACK AT AND REFRESH YOUR MEMORY AND ROUTINE. I CONSTANTLY POST THINGS ON SOCIAL MEDIA, SO MAKE SURE TO FOLLOW ME ON INSTAGRAM FOR MORE INFORMATION @TENNIS_HOUSTON

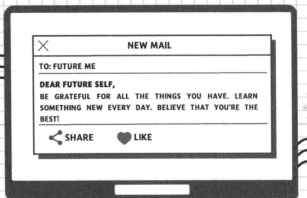

> **✕**   **NEW MAIL**
>
> TO: FUTURE ME
>
> **DEAR FUTURE SELF,**
> BE GRATEFUL FOR ALL THE THINGS YOU HAVE. LEARN SOMETHING NEW EVERY DAY. BELIEVE THAT YOU'RE THE BEST!
>
> 🔗 SHARE   ❤ LIKE

IF YOU FOUND THIS WORKBOOK HELPFUL AND LIKED THE LESSONS, PLEASE RECOMMEND IT TO YOUR FAMILY AND FRIENDS. IT ALSO MAKES A GREAT GIFT. PERHAPS, IT WILL INSPIRE SOMEBODY TO EXERCISE MORE OFTEN AND LIVE A HEALTHIER LIFESTYLE.

PLEASE COMPLETE THE SURVEY AND HELP ME TO IMPROVE THE LESSONS. YOUR FEEDBACK IS HIGHLY APPRECIATED.

THANK YOU, COACH NINA

Made in the USA
Las Vegas, NV
08 September 2023

77246853R00057